TECHNOCRACY TO TRIBULATION

By Fred DeRuvo

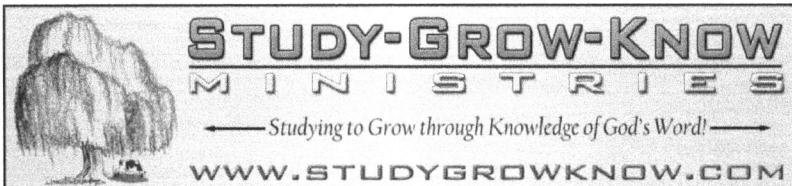

STUDY-GROW-KNOW
MINISTRIES
—— Studying to Grow through Knowledge of God's Word! ——
WWW.STUDYGROWKNOW.COM

Published in Scotts Valley, California, by Study-Grow-Know
www.studygrowknow.com • www.studygrowknowblog.com

Unless noted, Scripture quotations are from the New American Standard Bible, Copyright ©1960, 1962, 1963, 1968, 1971, 1972, 1973, 1975, 1977, 1995 by The Lockman Foundation.

All images unless otherwise noted were created by Fred DeRuvo. Cover concept by Fred DeRuvo. Cover images used (with permission): © Kwest - Fotolia.com

Photo of EU Parliament on page 9: Copyright: 123RF Stock Photo (Used with permission)

Edited by: Hannah Brady

Library of Congress Cataloging-in-Publication Data

DeRuvo, Fred, 1957 –

ISBN 0988183366
EAN-13 978-0-9881833-6-0

1. Religion – Eschatology

Contents

Fred DeRuvo is the author of numerous books and articles related to religious studies. He received his bachelor's degree from Philadelphia College of Bible, his master's from Tyndale Theological Seminary, and his Th.D. from Northwestern Theological Seminary in Florida.

Fred endeavors to share the good news of Christ's death and resurrection, which remains the only viable atonement for sinful humanity, in order that we might become God's adopted children by receiving salvation.

Listen to Dr. Fred's weekly audio program Study-Grow-Know at:

www.SermonAudio.com/studygrowknow

Smartphone apps are also available for download for **iPhones** and **Android**-based phones. Check with the app store for your particular phone.

"Because lawlessness is increased, most people's love will grow cold."

– Matthew 24:12

There are many things in the world that are completely evil. In fact, though God is ultimately in control, this world seems too often to be governed by evil. It is so because Satan is the god of this age (cf. 2 Corinthians 4:4), the ruler of this world (John 13:30), and he is also the ruler of the powers of the air (cf. Ephesians 2:2).

Interestingly enough, the people who give themselves over to Satan to be used of him for what they believe to be personal gain seem to defy any type of logic at all. They appear to be completely devoid of any real humanity, so united are they in purpose with Satan.

Satan hates humanity and we must never forget that. We are dealing with an enemy who exists to *destroy*. While he was not always like that, once sin was found within him, not only was his eternal destiny decided, but humanity's was changed.

Numerous authors speak of the coming "Technocracy" and the "Technocrats" behind it who are creating a world that will be one in purpose and mindset. It will be a world guided not by the rule of law, but one guided by the weight of **regulations**. These regulations will not be set in stone, either. Instead, they will be constantly tweaked for the best outcome by the new "priests" of the day, scientists and engineers.

All of this will be controlled by the Technocrats (global elite, power elite, globalists, Illuminati, etc.) because they will come to have the ultimate power since they currently have most of the world's wealth. They believe their day to rule as kings over this earth is coming and the Bible would agree, for ten of them at least (Revelation 17).

However, what they fail to see is that their rule will be short-lived and will ultimately *fail*. They are being allowed to bring this world to global governance not for themselves, but for Satan himself, though they are ignorant of that fact. Satan will have every chance to bring his promises of Isaiah 14 to fruition. He will attempt this through his spiritual son Antichrist, who will be the *visible* display of Satan's tremendous, albeit *limited*, power.

This will occur during the coming Tribulation, which is brought about because of the sins of the world and the globalists who move the world toward their dreamed-of Utopia. They have pushed God from His rightful place, replacing Him with the god of science. How they have been working to accomplish this is what this book is about.

Since the late 1950s, the decade in which I was born, life has undergone tremendous changes and, if anything, those changes are speeding up so that more change happens more quickly. We could almost say that a new system of Babylon (unlike the physical structure of Genesis 11) is being built right under our noses, and because of that, the effect it has had and continues to have on society is thoroughly evil.

What are all the things that have occurred in society that are so much different from when I was a kid, and maybe when you were as well? In this book, we'll see exactly how Satan has been at work building a system that is ultimately meant to enslave everyone in the world, with few exceptions. No one – especially Christians – will be untouched.

Whether we're speaking of the "Smart Grid" that is connecting all of us via a very unique Wi-Fi to a very complex computerized matrix, aspects of the Emergent Church, or the food we eat, control of virtually every aspect of society is in the works.

It may seem a bit strange to be discussing problems with our food supply, but consider that many food companies are owned by corporations that also own pharmaceutical companies. Is there a problem? We'll investigate to determine whether or not globalists have reached into the food supply in order to make it impossible for us to live a healthy lifestyle.

Can we see the New Babylon at work today and can we gain a greater grasp of just what things actually look like as we move toward the Tribulation?

In essence, this book – *Technocracy to Tribulation* – takes us below the surface to see what is being created right under our very noses, yet out of sight. The result will be a thoroughly godless and lawless system that will be ruled by the "man of lawlessness" himself, as referenced by the apostle Paul in 2 Thessalonians 2.

The Bible is roughly two-thirds prophecy, with about one-third not yet fulfilled. We are living in an age and time when we may well see some of the disturbing events the Bible showcases. These events occur for a purpose and, ultimately, that purpose is to glorify God. It is my hope that this book will open your eyes to what God has planned for the future of this planet. May He alone be glorified.

Fred DeRuvo, May 2015

Chapter 1

The New Tower of Babel

D o you know that the new Tower of Babel is being constructed under our very noses? I'm not referring to the European Union's (EU) Parliamentarian building (shown next page) in Strasbourg, France, inspired by Pieter Bruegel's famous 16th century painting, "The Tower of Babel." Incidentally, the Tower of Babel was used on an EU poster printed up to highlight "Europe: Many Tongues, One Voice."

What I'm referring to is the *system* of Babylon that is literally being built behind the scenes and in the shadows, a system we are essentially powerless to stop. For one thing, we cannot *see* it being constructed. It is being created by people variously called *global-ists, global elite, power elite, the elite, Illuminati,* and the *oligar-chy*, as well as numerous other labels. We may as well call them *Technocrats* because the world is being moved toward a highly developed system based on *scientism* (worship of sci-ence). Author Patrick M. Wood refers to this as *Technocracy* in his book, "*Technocracy Rising.*"

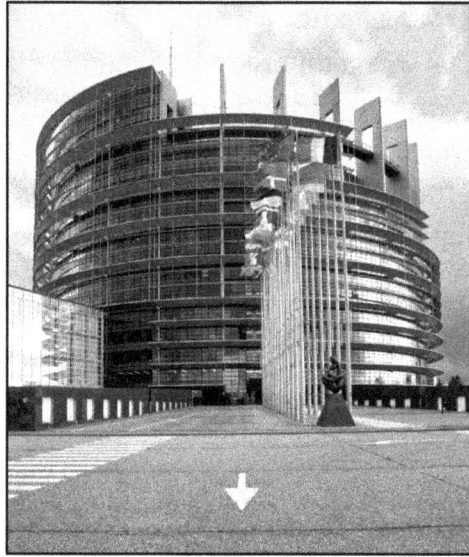

If we were to see a physical structure being built that seemed to attempt to reach the heavens like the original Tower of Babel (Genesis 11), Christians could focus our efforts on shutting it down. While we might still fail, our efforts would be focused on a physical, visible structure.

Unfortunately, that is not the case at all. Though the EU Parliamentarian building is an obvious representation of the Tower of Babel, the building itself has no power and no ability to deceive. It merely provides a nod or wink to the original Tower of Babel from Genesis 11.

That particular building – unlike the structure in Genesis 11 – has not gathered all people together under one purpose, language, and mission. However, it is clear that the building epitomizes what Technocrats believe and what they've been working toward building throughout the world since the late 1800s (and in earnest during more modern times).

The new Tower of Babel is an *ideology* – a theology, even – for people who are thoroughly caught up in rebellion against God, His created order, and His salvation. They are so desperate to become kings of this world that they are willing to do whatever it takes – via Technocracy – to develop an order in which they are their own gods, in which they decide how, when, and why to tweak a system so that it provides the best output...for *them* and their families. They are working to place all things under their control. It is happening.

Author Patrick M. Wood notes that today's new universal language is *digital*. Because of the computer age, and even though not everyone speaks the same language, the fluency with which people converse digitally has evened the playing field. Wood notes:

> *"[T]his is the new common language spoken by those who would build a modern Tower of Babel (i.e. Transhumanism) to displace God in the same manner as the account in Genesis 11. The clear implication of Prophecy today is that God will not deal with this current rebellion until the world enters the future 7-year period known as the Tribulation as described in the book of Revelation. The first rebellion ended in humanity being scattered throughout the world which was certainly inconvenient but not necessarily deadly. The second rebellion will end with all-consuming judgment."*[1]

What Satan was unable to accomplish the first time (because God halted the process due to His timing and purposes), he has worked to achieve since. It would appear that God is allowing Satan to create what he was unable to complete in Genesis 11. Of course, Satan has learned from his mistakes. He's not interested in pulling the world together to build a *physical* structure that attempts to reach to the heavens. For what purpose would that work? He has other ways, better ways to accomplish his purposes now.

---

[1] Patrick M. Wood, Technocracy Rising (2015), p. 212

Today's average unsaved individual couldn't care less about a physical structure like the Tower of Babel. Unlike those who lived during the days of Noah *after* the Flood and believed in some sort of very powerful deity, today's average person doesn't believe in the God of the Bible. Instead, they likely see themselves as some sort of deity, if they have any religious beliefs or affirmations at all. This person would have no interest in a physical structure as a focal point that directs his or her attention to the heavens. In reality, Satan has been directing people to see themselves as *gods*, therefore, an exterior physical structure is counterproductive for today's average lost person. The religion of today is *Humanistic Relativism*, or simply *Humanism*.

No, what Satan has been busily constructing (and using Technocrats to do it) is a largely invisible matrix that easily fits into any society on earth, whether Socialistic, Communistic, Democratic, or even a Constitutional Republic. Though in some cases that society will see some outward changes, many things can and do remain the same externally so that it does not appear to be all that different once Technocrats get hold of it and make the sought-after changes.

This can be clearly seen in China today since Technocrats via their corporations got into China during the Carter administration. Nothing in China has really changed simply because of the already existing suppression of rights that existed *before* these Technocrats became part of the picture. Certainly, the average worker in China does not benefit from the presence of these large corporations. These workers are merely cheap labor, without union protection.

Many of the changes (and attempted changes) within the United States have also been accomplished via Technocrats and their system of Technocracy. Their ultimate goal, of course, is to create a world where they rule. This is why it appears so odd to us that President

Obama has opened the door to Cuba, an "enemy" of America.[2] Yet, as stated, under Jimmy Carter, the door was thrown wide open to China so that a normalized relationship (think *trade,* equaling *profits* for corporations) could be achieved. It's all about what Technocrats want and they want to increase their profits to gain more control.

Technocrats ultimately want freedom to do whatever they think best in a global society, for their own purposes. To this end, they will not only find ways to maximize profits for themselves but will also find a way to outlaw guns and limit free speech in America. They will force their will on all nations once they can get past the dreaded *rule of law* in countries like the US. They've been consistently whittling away at it for decades and they don't have too much further to go in order to fully succeed.

Technocrats govern by rules and regulations. This is why the presidential executive order has been used and abused not just by President Obama, but by presidents going back to FDR. It's not that Obama hates America. That may well be the case, but that's not the point. The point is that Obama (like many presidents before him), works for Technocrats to fulfill the Technocratic vision of the future.

The new Tower of Babel – as a largely hidden system – is being built *secretly,* and it would not surprise me to see it come to fruition in all its fullness one day soon. In essence, the world is being forced to accept and adopt the tenets of Technocracy, which is in reality the new Tower of Babel.

Technocracy rules out God in favor of science. We are being taught that only through science can our planet be saved. Wealth needs to be redistributed (though not the Technocrats' wealth), and shared so that the poor have what those who are not poor already have (even though they gained it through hard work).

---

[2] http://www.usatoday.com/story/news/politics/2014/12/17/obama-cuba-alan-gross-prisoner/20526497/ (05/22/2015)

But do you for one moment believe that the Technocrats who have the lion's share of wealth on this planet will share *any* of theirs? Of course not. They want to simply take from those who have and give to those who have not, so that everyone in society (except them) will be on an even playing field. They will stand above the rest of us as rulers.

It's not necessarily a Socialist program that is being adopted (though in many ways, it *looks* like that). What *is* being adopted is a Technocracy or system of governance that will guide every aspect of humanity. The only ones who will be exempt from Technocracy will be those who *control* it and that's always the way it has been.

Think of the people who are in charge of the EU today. They were *not* elected to their posts. They were *appointed*. They are the movers and shakers and policy makers who decide (through *regulations*, much like the executive order) what happens in the EU, who gets what, and how it all works. They *are* the law because they *make* the law without the consent or input of the people. Consider Greece – a democracy – a country that has literally been taken over by Technocrat regulators, supposedly all for the good of the "whole" (not Greece, but the EU).

This is what is coming to the United States, and based on what Scripture tells us, we will not be able to stop it. At best, we might throw a monkey wrench in things at the local level, but nothing more. The Technocrats will rule through the Technocratic society they are being allowed (by God) to create, using Satan's energy and power.

This is the new Tower of Babel and the coming Tribulation is meant in part as judgment against this new "tower" that attempts to dethrone God, turning His Creation on its head, while at the same time, elevating science to that of godhood.

Technocracy is "*a government or social system controlled by techni-cians, especially scientists and technical experts.*"[3] What we are seeing in America and the world today is a push by Technocrats to move the world toward a system of governance whereby that entire world is controlled by a cadre of scientists, engineers, and other experts.

It is clear that humanity's movement *towards* a Technocracy is the direct result of man's obstinate flight *away* from God. There will come a point when God's patience will end and His judgment in wrath will begin. That time is the coming Tribulation, and though one specific event will start the coming Tribulation (that event is *not* the Rapture), in many ways, the start of the Tribulation is the culmina-tion of thousands of years of humanity's rebellion toward God.

What will make all of this possible is the advance of technology in which man has removed God from His rightful place as Ruler, having replaced Him with *science*. Scientism – or the worship of science – is firmly established as god for humanity. Through it, it is believed that there are no limits to what man can accomplish.

Though not all people throughout the earth speak the same oral lan-guage, science is universal. The concepts that undergird it are under-stood across all cultures. Because of man's dependence on science, God is no longer needed. Man now possesses the power to do what-ever his mind can imagine.

God will not be mocked. He will not be ignored. He *will* be seen as the only God who is above all things. Science cannot replace God because it is a tool that man uses to discover truth. Unfortunately, the limit to science is found in man's own limitations and the limitations of the dimensions in which we live and operate.

The coming Tribulation will occur because humanity will bring this world to that point by playing god while endeavoring to ignore the

---

[3] http://www.thefreedictionary.com/technocracy (03/06/2015)

only true God. He has stated that He will not share His glory (cf. Isaiah 42:8), yet man has tried repeatedly to claim some of that glory, as has Satan.

The Tribulation signals the fact that God will allow man to do his worst, and even with all of Satan's power working through him, man will fail miserably. The only salvation that exists is the one found not in man's ability, but in God's.

The Tribulation period that is coming is the time when God's wrath pours out on humanity. This will be done in an effort to humble humanity to the point where each person is willing and able to understand that there is one God.

Unfortunately, as we shall see, many to most will stubbornly reject God, even when their rebellion against Him is seen for what it is and they realize that not only can they not fight against Him, but they cannot even stand in His Presence.

Chapter 2

Tribulation vs. THE Tribulation

T he specifics of *the* coming Tribulation are taught in Scripture, and the Tribulation Jesus spoke of in Matthew 24, among other places, includes a series of judgments from God's throne to those who reside on earth. This coming time of Tribulation – lasting seven years, according to Scripture – is *still* in the future.

To be clear, this book is not meant as an exhaustive study on the subject of the coming Tribulation. It is meant to provide basic details concerning this coming time when the world will experience what Jesus says will be the greatest tribulation the world will have ever known. In other words, we haven't arrived to it...yet.

When considering the Tribulation, it is important to understand that the first half of the Tribulation is written about by John the apostle in the book of Revelation, 6:1 – 9:21. Revelation 10:1 – 14:20 highlight the middle of the Tribulation, and the second half of the Tribulation is discussed in Revelation 15:1 – 16:21.

Because there is currently such tremendous persecution of Christians throughout the world, as well as other things that *seem* to remind us of certain plagues of the Tribulation period, many articles and books published today state that either the Tribulation has already happened or that we are currently in it now. I believe that both of these positions are erroneous. I fully believe that the entirety of the Tribulation – all seven years of it – is still in front of us.

While at times we may be tempted to believe that the actual Tribulation has begun, I believe the Bible provides a clear picture of when the Tribulation will actually begin. I do *not* mean that we can determine the day or hour that it begins. I simply mean that, based on the events in Scripture, we can determine what happens prior to the start of the Tribulation, and in fact, we can also determine the exact event that kicks it off, though knowing this puts us no closer to figuring out dates and times when the Tribulation is slated to begin.

The word "tribulation" is used in Scripture in several ways. First, it is used in a general way to note that life is often replete with difficulties (tribulations) that vex us, that try our faith. If we allow them, these seasons of tribulation will cause us to *grow* in our faith. They are ordained by God and it is our job to humble ourselves under His mighty hand so that in due time He will lift us up (cf. 1 Peter 5:6).

Second, the word "tribulation" is also used in a very specific way to point to a time set by the Lord Himself and has come to be known as THE Tribulation period. Context can and often does make the difference in understanding exactly how a word or phrase is used in Scripture.

For instance, Paul, in his letter to the Romans, stated this about general tribulations: "*And not only this, but we also exult in our tribulations, knowing that tribulation brings about perseverance...*" (Romans 5:3). Paul is speaking here of the general difficulties that everyone, including Christians, experiences in this life because of the fall.

James points to the same thing in James 1:2-4, when he states, "*Consider it all joy, my brethren, when you encounter various trials, knowing that the testing of your faith produces endurance. And let endurance have its perfect result, so that you may be perfect and complete, lacking in nothing.*" The type of tribulation James speaks of *can* include persecution that comes from the world (ultimately, Satan). God often uses this type of persecution to strengthen our resolve, our faith, and our testimony to the world. He uses it to build us up.

However, there is a huge difference between this type of general tribulation (also referred to as trials) noted by Paul, James, and others, and the *specific* Tribulation period that Jesus points to in the Olivet Discourse. There, in Matthew 24, Jesus points to a specific period of time toward the end of this current age in which we live when, because of the fact that God will pour out His judgment on the earth in the form of wrath-filled judgments, the world will be a terrible place. More detail is provided in the chart on the following page.

It seems clear that many of the things mentioned in the chart have happened in history since nearly the beginning of time. History is replete with wars, rumors of wars, pestilences, famines, international discord, and certainly persecution and martyrdom. However, it is just as clear that Jesus stated these things *will* occur in greater frequency and intensity during the time leading directly up to the final seven years of this age, or what is known as the Tribulation period.

In Jesus' Olivet Discourse, He warns repeatedly just how bad things will become during that time. It will be as though hell itself unleashes all of its power on earth and those who are alive at that time. Of

EVENT	Rev 6	Matt 24	Mark 13	Luke 21
False messiahs, false prophets	6:2	24:5, 11	13:6	21:8
Wars	6:2-4	24:6-7	13:7	21:9
Int'l discord	6:3-4	24:7	13:8	21:10
Famines	6:5-8	24:7	13:8	21:11
Pestilences	6:8			21:11
Persecution, martyrdom	6:9-11	24:9	13:9-13	21:12-17
Earthquakes	6:12	24:7	13:8	21:11
Cosmic phenomenon	6:12-14	24:29	13:24-25	21:11

Table based on *A Testimony of Jesus Christ, Volume 1*, Dr. Tony Garland, 2004, p 145

course, all of these things regarding the timing, ferocity, and length will be controlled by God Himself.

This upcoming time period is designated to be a time of God's wrath for good reason. If we look at Daniel 9:27, we will clearly see that the final "week" (seven years) of human history begins when the "he" in that verse confirms a *covenant* with the many for one week. The "he" in that verse points to the Antichrist (going back to the first antecedent, being the "prince" of the people who is to come in verse 26b; not Messiah, but the other "prince" referenced in the text).

This coming Antichrist will confirm some type of covenant with the many (referring here to Israel; the entire context of the 9th chapter of Daniel refers to the people of Israel, or Daniel's people). Once Antichrist does that, Israel will have effectively signed a deal with the devil (literally) and it is at that point that God's patience with His created nation and chosen people comes to an end. The refining will now begin in earnest.

We note that in Revelation 5 and following, all activity related to the Tribulation period (the final "week" of human history referenced in Daniel 9:27) is directed by the Lamb from heaven's throne. Satan is merely one of the chief players in the unfolding events of that period.

We need to understand then that this specific Tribulation that Jesus refers to in Matthew 24 is the set period of time referenced in Daniel 9:27 (and various other places throughout Scripture). There are specific reasons why God has decreed that this period of seven years will occur as the Tribulation/Great Tribulation. Please note the image on the next page that supplies the reasons for this coming period of Tribulation, as noted in Daniel 9:24-27. They are as follows:

1. *To finish the transgression (which is tied to the rejection of Messiah)*
2. *To make an end of sin*
3. *To make reconciliation for iniquity*
4. *To bring in an age of righteousness*
5. *To cause a cessation of prophecy*
6. *To anoint the Most Holy Place*

The above reasons highlight *why* the Tribulation will occur. It will allow God to pull out and perfect the final remnant of those within the nation of Israel. It will be those Jews – that final remnant – who will live through the Tribulation period and be welcomed into the Millennial Kingdom ruled by Jesus Himself. During that Millennial Kingdom, these Jews will – as the representatives of the nation of Israel – enjoy *all* the Land that was originally promised to Israel via Abraham. This is the main reason for the coming Tribulation/Great Tribulation. It is important to understand this.

The Beginning of the Great Tribulation from Daniel 9:24-27

Six Purposes of Seventy Sevens

Decree from God

"Seventy weeks are decreed upon your people and upon your holy city,..."
Daniel 9:24a

| To Finish the Transgression (Rejection of Messiahship) | To Make an End of Sins | To Make Reconciliation for Iniquity | To Bring in an Age of Righteousness | To Cause a Cessation of Prophecy | To Anoint the Most Holy Place |

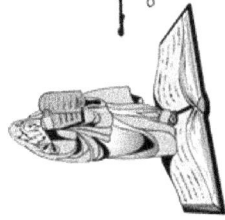

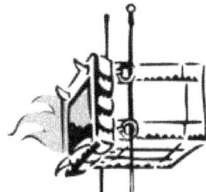

But the Tribulation is also the time that God has chosen to pour out His wrath onto the nations that have rejected Him, God the Savior, *and* His chosen people of Israel.

From beginning to end, the entirety of the seven years represents God's wrath. We will spend time in this book looking at many of the aspects of the Tribulation period, when it begins, what happens during that period of time, and the events leading up to it.

Chapter 3

What About the Rapture?

The plain fact of the matter is that the coming seven-year period known as the Tribulation does *not* begin with the Rapture. Let's get that out of the way right from the start of things. In fact, the Tribulation has nothing *directly* to do with the Rapture, and *vice versa*.

While this author firmly believes that the Bible teaches a PreTrib Rapture (a gathering together of all authentic Christians to the Lord in the air according to 1 Thessalonians 4; cf. also 2 Thessalonians 2), the beginning of the Tribulation has nothing to do with the Rapture at all directly. However, there *are* some *indirect* connections.

There are some things that will most certainly advance in society due to the fact that the Rapture occurs, but the Rapture could happen today, while the start of the Tribulation could be a month, a year, five years or more down the road. The two events are *not* directly connected.

At the same time, it needs to be stated that the *results* of the PreTrib Rapture, including the immediate and long-term aftermath, are extremely important in bringing society to the point where the Tribulation will begin. It is essential to understand this.

In 1 Thessalonians 4, Paul teaches (and refers again to it in 2 Thessalonians 2), that the coming Rapture of the invisible Church is *PreTrib* in nature. That is, the Rapture will occur *prior* to the Tribulation, and there are numerous reasons that this makes sense, both biblically and extra-biblically.

Many books have been written on the subject of the Rapture with presentations from all sides. Of late – probably within the past 20 to 30 years – those who reject the PreTrib Rapture position have gone to the extent of attacking both the position itself and those who hold it. The people making the attacks believe that their anger and accompanying vitriol is born of a "righteous indignation." They firmly believe that those who hold such a position – that the Rapture will occur *prior* to the Tribulation – are deceiving many because they themselves are also deceived.

This alleged deception is one they believe will cause people to fall away from the faith. They also argue that when the Tribulation begins and the Rapture has not happened yet, the people who have been deceived into believing the PreTrib Rapture position will – because of their entrenched deception – end up taking the mark of the beast and will spend eternity without Christ. The absurdity of this is evident when realizing that the sealing of the Holy Spirit, His indwelling nature, and the fact that Jesus is the Author and Perfecter of our faith, are all set aside based on a straw man argument.

Of course, this also means that the individuals who believe this also believe that salvation can be lost or rejected; something this author does not believe the Scriptures teach. The entire argument against PreTrib Rapturists has become thoroughly problematic because it pits Christian against Christian and the entire process of evangelism stops. It has arisen due to several completely man-made arguments that, in themselves, appear to negate the clear teaching of Scripture.

Look around the Internet and you will see website after website dedicated solely to critiquing and condemning the "false teaching/deception" of PreTrib Rapturism. That is the entire focus and these people inordinately believe that their calling to evangelize starts and stops with people who have been "deceived" into believing the PreTrib Rapture. It is patently obscene to believe that God in Christ has no more control over those who are His than these particular individuals give Him credit for having. In essence, they are robbing God of His power and ability to *keep* those who trust in Him.

This author has dealt with the subject of the Rapture in articles and books and has presented a complete and fairly thorough discourse on why the PreTrib Rapture is the only plausible way to understand Paul's teaching.[4] Because of that, there is no point in presenting that same information here. Instead, information that is specific to Paul's teaching in either 1 or 2 Thessalonians with the Tribulation in view will be presented. Readers are encouraged to do their own study of God's Word to determine through prayer and humble submission to the Lord which view of the Rapture is the correct view.

Admittedly, due to the constant "blame and shame" game from those who stand in opposition to the PreTrib Rapture, many have backed

---

[4] Fred DeRuvo, *The PreTrib Rapture* (2009) as one example.

off from discussion of the PreTrib Rapture. The amount of abject vitriol, negativity, and personal attack has made it easier to avoid the subject because a person's salvation does not hinge upon it, though some clearly believe it does.

However, the Bible does *not* avoid the subject, and IF the PreTrib Rapture occurs prior to the start of the Tribulation, then saints living during that period of time will surely be blessed because of it. The rest of us will die physically *first* but will also participate in the Rapture (the *dead* in Christ will rise first, as declared by Paul in 1 Thessalonians 4:16). Let's look at the text.

> *"But we do not want you to be uninformed, brethren, about those who are asleep, so that you will not grieve as do the rest who have no hope. For if we believe that Jesus died and rose again, even so God will bring with Him those who have fallen asleep in Jesus. For this we say to you by the word of the Lord, that we who are alive and remain until the coming of the Lord, will not precede those who have fallen asleep. For the Lord Himself will descend from heaven with a shout, with the voice of the archangel and with the trumpet of God, and the dead in Christ will rise first. Then we who are alive and remain will be caught up together with them in the clouds to meet the Lord in the air, and so we shall always be with the Lord. Therefore comfort one another with these words"* (1 Thessalonians 4:13-18).

In the above verses, Paul speaks of an event we call the Rapture. The phrase or term he uses in the text is *"caught up,"* which in the Latin translates to *"rapture"* in English. This is clearly not the Second Coming, though some read into the Scripture here by saying that when the Lord "descends," He descends all the way to the earth. Yet, this is not stated or truly implied in this section of Scripture at all. It is simply understood that way by those who believe that the Rapture happens at the exact same time as the Lord's physical Second Coming (at the end of the Tribulation period).

This is what Paul is commenting on or reminding the believers at Thessalonica about in his second letter to them. He does not want them to be afraid that the Rapture has already occurred or that the "day of the Lord" (beginning with the start of the Tribulation), has already taken place.

So is it pointless then to even discuss the Rapture if, for instance, the Rapture is a long way off (even if it is *PreTribulational*)? No, and in fact, as we study the Bible concerning the times leading up to and including the Tribulation period, we learn exactly the type of impact the PreTrib Rapture has on society throughout the globe when it happens and how it actually helps bring about the "mystery of lawlessness" that Paul refers to in 2 Thessalonians 2.

In that section of Scripture, Paul refers to this "mystery of lawlessness" that will exist *prior* to the start of the Tribulation. In fact, though we know that this same lawlessness was alive and well during Paul's day, it is obviously very clear that it has progressed to the point where, roughly 2,000 years later, it has become even *more* palpably evil than it was during Paul's lifetime because it has gained a stronger foothold throughout the earth.

This lawlessness that Paul speaks of is intended to *capture* the world's attention prior to the arrival and revealing of Antichrist *and* the start of the Tribulation period. Let's look at the text of 2 Thessalonians 2:1-12 to see what we can see.

> *"1 Now we request you, brethren, with regard to the coming of our Lord Jesus Christ and our gathering together to Him, 2 that you not be quickly shaken from your composure or be disturbed either by a spirit or a message or a*

letter as if from us, to the effect that the day of the Lord has come.

"3 Let no one in any way deceive you, for it will not come unless the apostasy comes first, and the man of lawlessness is revealed, the son of destruction, 4 who opposes and exalts himself above every so-called god or object of worship, so that he takes his seat in the temple of God, displaying himself as being God.

"5 Do you not remember that while I was still with you, I was telling you these things? 6 And you know what restrains him now, so that in his time he will be revealed. 7 For the mystery of lawlessness is already at work; only he who now restrains will do so until he is taken out of the way.

"8 Then that lawless one will be revealed whom the Lord will slay with the breath of His mouth and bring to an end by the appearance of His coming; 9 that is, the one whose coming is in accord with the activity of Satan, with all power and signs and false wonders, 10 and with all the deception of wickedness for those who perish, because they did not receive the love of the truth so as to be saved.

"11 For this reason God will send upon them a deluding influence so that they will believe what is false, 12 in order that they all may be judged who did not believe the truth, but took pleasure in wickedness."

Verse 1 references the fact that authentic Christians will be *gathered together* at His coming. This is important verbiage to understand. According to Dr. Thomas Constable, "*The Lord's 'appearance' (Gr. epiphaneia) is a different and later event in His 'coming' (Gr. parousia)* than the 'gathering' (Gr. episynagoges) event (v. 1). The first event is the Rapture, and the second is the Second Coming."[5]

In verse 2, Paul then provides comfort for those who have been "shaken" by reports that the "day of the Lord" (or "day of Christ") has already begun or is ready to start. In verse 3, Paul backs up his statement with a context, indicating that the coming "day of the Lord" (which starts with and includes the Tribulation period) cannot happen unless there is a "falling away" first. This must occur because it is this "mystery of lawlessness" that drives the world to the point where the Tribulation must begin because of global deception.

Regarding this "falling away" (or *apostasy*), *"...it seems likely that the apostasy Paul had in mind expanded on Jewish apocalyptic expectations and envisioned a dramatic and climactic falling away from the worship of the true God (by both Jews and some portion of the Christian church) as a part of the complex of events at the end of the age."*[6]

Paul appears to be stating that the "mystery of lawlessness" will build to a point where a great falling away occurs, then "he" who keeps things in check will be moved out of the way. There is, of course, great debate over the identify of this "he" is in that passage, but it seems clear enough that the "he" is the Holy Spirit working through the *invisible* Church. Once the Church is removed, the Holy Spirit will not be able to work through that avenue; though of course the Holy Spirit is still here, working to accomplish all of God's purposes, but just no longer through the Church.

The falling away that Paul speaks of, though alive and growing during Paul's day, will become so incredibly thorough in all of society prior to the beginnings of the Tribulation (and will continue as a crescendo right up to the time Jesus physically returns at the end of the Tribulation), that it will be as though there is no restraint on society at all.

---

[5] http://soniclight.com/constable/notes/pdf/2thessalonians.pdf, p. 14
[6] http://soniclight.com/constable/notes/pdf/2thessalonians.pdf, p. 14

> *"When the Rapture takes place, and all true Christians
> leave the earth, this great 'apostasy,' which is connected
> with a worldwide delusion or deception, will overwhelm
> the human race."*[7]

We need to stop and think about the *ramifications* of the PreTrib
Rapture. While some have spent their time harping about the alleged
deception that they believe undergirds the PreTrib Rapture belief,
they seem to have missed several extremely cogent points that are
connected to this event.

It is very important to understand that the Tribulation does not take
place in a vacuum but *coincides* with events that occur in society. This
is all part of God's timing and purposes. In essence, the occurrence of
the Rapture allows for the *worsening* of society. That is part of its
purpose, much like God locking Noah and his family in the Ark allowed for the rains and floods to begin.

Besides the constant push toward evil that currently exists in global
society, certain events highlighted in the Bible will play their part in
allowing and advocating a greater advance of evil than would have
occurred had those events *not* happened at all. Certainly one large,
unmistakable event is the Rapture. Yet, too many people tend to
think of the Rapture as merely an event in which millions of authentic Christians are taken off the planet. That is certainly part of it – one
side of the coin. However, the other side of the coin – the *result* of the
Rapture occurring – is represented by the things that occur in society
because the Rapture has taken place. This cannot be stressed enough.

In order for the Tribulation to begin, global society will have to reach
a point where the level of evil becomes so great that reversing direction back to God is impossible. The restructuring of society through
its continued conforming to evil pushes society away from God to an

---

[7] http://soniclight.com/constable/notes/pdf/2thessalonians.pdf, p. 15

ever-increasing degree. This causes a growing number of people to embrace an increasing level of evil.

Once the Rapture has occurred, the restraining influence of the Holy Spirit in and through the Church will be gone (since the Church will be gone). This extremely important event leaves a vacuum in society that causes evil to rush in and fill it. This is something that most opposed to the PreTrib Rapture do not seem to recognize.

Even though Paul does not mention the Rapture in verses 3 and 4 of 2 Thessalonians 2 (though he *does* refer to it in 1 Thessalonians 4:13-18, while *alluding* to it in 2 Thessalonians 2), it is clear that it is part of the discussion. While he does not present a chronological order of events here (but more of a *logical* one, in which the Rapture is included but not specifically mentioned, based on what he taught in 1 Thessalonians 4:13-18), it is understood that the Rapture is obviously part of the equation.

Based on what Paul taught the Thessalonian believers (as referenced in 1 Thessalonians), *if* the Tribulation had already begun, then either 1) the Rapture had occurred and believers at Thessalonica were left behind, or 2) the Rapture didn't happen because they had misunderstood Paul's clear teaching on the matter. In any case, Paul wanted to calm their fears, once again reminding them that there is a logical progression of events that will lead up to and include all of the Tribulation.

First and foremost, a falling away must occur, then the man of sin will be revealed (*after* this falling away, at some point during the Tribulation), and this same man of sin will end up in the Lake of Fire (to receive his eternal destruction). The reason Paul doesn't deal again with the Rapture here is because he is specifically being asked about the "day of the Lord," and in this context, the Rapture is not included in that "day." The Rapture is a completely separate event in which all authentic Christians are "caught up" to be with the Lord forever *before* the Tribulation begins.

This is not something that the true Church brings about or is in any way *active* in. The true Christians who make up the invisible Church are *taken up* to be with the Lord. This demonstrates a *passive* participation of true Christians in this event. We have nothing to do with it other than to be carried off to meet the Lord in the air. We cannot make the Rapture happen when we want it to occur. We cannot live in such a way as to make the Rapture happen sooner. The timing of the Rapture is set by God in His timetable. We cannot make it happen sooner than it is planned to occur.

Moreover, Christians won't be *actively* involved in the Rapture when it does take place, any more than dirt and dust sucked up by a vacuum cleaner is *active* in the vacuuming process (to use a poor example). This is important to understand.

> *"At the rapture the church is 'caught up' or 'snatched away,' an event wherein the Lord acts to transport believers from earth into His presence (1 Thess. 4:16-17). Everything that takes place with the believers at the rapture is initiated by the Lord and done by Him. Paul has just referred to the rapture as 'our gathering together unto him' (v. 1); why then should he now use this unlikely term to mean the same thing?"*[8]

Even though the world – prior to the Tribulation (and the Rapture) – will be experiencing ever-increasing *apostasy*, it will not be until *after* the Rapture that this "falling away" or "apostasy" can increase tremendously. Why? Paul provides the answer in 2 Thessalonians 2:7-8.

---

[8] http://soniclight.com/constable/notes/pdf/2thessalonians.pdf, p. 15

> *"7 For the mystery of lawlessness is already at work; only he who now restrains will do so until he is taken out of the way.*

> *"8 Then that lawless one will be revealed whom the Lord will slay with the breath of His mouth and bring to an end by the appearance of His coming"*

The "he" who is taken out of the way is the Holy Spirit. While some disagree and prefer other identities (such as Michael the Archangel, etc.), it seems that the text makes more sense if we understand that the Holy Spirit, who has been working in and through the Church since its inception in Acts 2, has been the One who has kept evil at bay so that it has not become as bad as it could become. This section of Scripture certainly does not mean that the Holy Spirit is taken out of the world. How could that be if God is omnipresent all the time?

What Paul seems to be referring to is the Holy Spirit's *influence* in the world through the invisible Church. Currently, authentic Christians who make up the Body of Christ (the Church) offer resistance to the enemy of our souls. The pressure that the very presence of true Christians places on the world through the moral climate of the Church itself is enough to keep evil from being purely evil.

Like Israel was intended to be, Christians are the light of this world namely because God, via the Holy Spirit, lives within us and has sealed us unto the day of redemption. Our life – because of God's presence within us – offers some measure of resistance against the wiles of the devil. The more committed we are to God, His purposes, and His glory, the greater our resistance and witness to the world.

This is exactly why Jesus told His disciples that the world hated Him and will also hate us. The world (prompted by Satan) hates us because of the fact that God lives within us. This is truth we need to absorb even though we do not live life perfectly here as Christians.

So consider what life will be like once the invisible (true) Church is taken out of this world. The Holy Spirit will no longer have the Church to work in and through. In *that* sense then He is taken out of the way. Though He obviously remains in the world and convicts the world of sin (people *do* become saved during the Tribulation), He works from the outside, as He did during the Old Testament times, rather than as He does now, with the Church present.

Once the Church is gone, it will be as though the dam that held back millions and millions of gallons of water has been removed. The water that was held back now surges ahead, destroying/affecting everything in its path. This will be what it looks like once the Rapture occurs. Imagine society at that point, considering how bad and corrupt it is *now*.

The Holy Spirit, through the Church, holds back the power of evil (like all the water behind the dam), but when God removes the Church, the Holy Spirit will no longer have that body of believers to work through. He will still get the job done, of course, but it will be done differently, and evil being thoroughly evil, will now be allowed to run amok in society, doing whatever damage it can.

The PreTrib Rapture is an event that is fully directed by God and simply acts upon all authentic Christians in society at that point. The event does not stop there, though.

While Christians are removed from society, the devastating effects will be seen in how much more rampant and unchecked evil becomes throughout society. This will greatly increase the evil, which will increase the level of apostasy, which will move the world toward the time when the man of sin/man of lawlessness will be revealed and the Tribulation can begin.

If the Church was left to remain in the world, the ramping up of evil to the point of a worldwide, cataclysmic, unchecked apostasy would not take place.

> "*In classical Greek the word apostasia denoted a political or military rebellion; but in the Greek Old Testament we find it used of rebellion against God (e.g. Jos. xxii. 22), and this becomes the accepted Biblical usage. Paul's thought is that in the last times there will be an outstanding mani-festation of the powers of evil arrayed against God.*"[9]

Regarding this coming *apostasia*, Dr. Thomas Constable notes that it "*does not mean simply disbelieving, but an aggressive and positive re-volt (cf. Acts 21:21; Heb. 3:12).*"[10] Too many include only Christians with this concept and see the entire realm of Christendom "depart-ing" from the faith. This is where they also include the belief that Christians can lose their salvation.

The reality is that it is very likely that Paul is including *all* of society in his warning here. If we consider the fact that in America alone, prayer and the Ten Commandments were removed from schools by the Supreme Court in the 1960s, and abortion on demand became the law of the land later in the 1970s, we clearly see an ongoing de-parture from the biblical tenets that were part of the founding docu-ments of America via our founding fathers.

Just over 200 years after the founding of America, we have seen God replaced with Humanism. The absolute truth of the Ten Command-ments has been replaced with emotional virtue (political correctness, aka Cultural Marxism), and murder (abortion) has become widely accepted as a means of "birth control."

---

[9] http://soniclight.com/constable/notes/pdf/2thessalonians.pdf, p. 14
[10] Ibid, p. 14

Society has been determined to move away from God and His absolute truth under the direction of Satan. This ultimately began in the Garden of Eden and continued during Paul's day when even then, truth had become relative (cf. John 18:38, when Pontius Pilate asks rhetorically, "what is truth?").

Today, some 2,000 years following the life, death, and resurrection of Jesus Christ, society clings in desperation to its desire to throw off God's chains (Psalm 2). The intentions of people have become far more pronounced and desperate.

The level of corruption in society and especially within the federal government of America, as well as governments of other nations, is astounding. There appears little hope of going back to the days before Humanism took its toll.

All of this has occurred even though the Holy Spirit has been working in and through His chosen vehicle, the true Church. But God's emphasis has always been on saving *souls*, not saving *nations* necessarily, though He will focus His efforts on Israel toward the end of this age prior to the return of Jesus (Matthew 24, Mark 13, Luke 21, Romans 9-11, etc.). In the meantime, the Holy Spirit's presence in the world (especially through the true Church) keeps evil at bay, while continuing to bring the lost into the invisible Church.

Once the Holy Spirit steps aside, the evil that He has withstood for eons will flow without remorse into the world, where it will create the greatest apostasy this world will have ever known. If the Rapture does not occur, this *cannot* happen.

The Rapture, while an extremely important future event, does several things, but it does *not* begin the Tribulation at all. By its nature, the Rapture will allow the evil that is currently being held in check loose to exploit the world and fill society with ever-increasing evil until the apostasy becomes so prevalent that the Tribulation can begin.

The Rapture has a *dual* purpose. It not only removes the true Church from this earth but also signals the go-ahead to the evil that will culminate in the apostasy that Paul speaks of in 2 Thessalonians 2.

Chapter 4

Unprecedented Evil

As we have discussed, the Rapture – if it occurs *prior* to the coming Tribulation as we believe it will – not only removes all true Christians from this world, but its occurrence will also enable global society to move that much more quickly toward the Tribulation period. This does not mean that society will be *forcing* the Tribulation to begin faster. It simply means that in God's plans and purposes, He has included this pace in the timing of His events.

The Tribulation period will begin due to several things occurring in society, but of course, it will ultimately start due to God's timing. First, as we have noted, Paul tells of a tremendous societal "falling away" (apostasy) that *will* occur. It is obvious from Paul's writings to the believers in Thessalonica that the Rapture of the invisible Church (made up only of *authentic* Christians, not those who are professing to be Christian but actually remain *lost*), will have an unmistakable effect on global society. It allows for the apostasy to occur (which has already begun in society throughout the world), and gain momentum.

There is no way that the Rapture can take place without directly impacting the world. That is completely *illogical* in all respects. It is that such a tremendous level of apostasy can occur if the Holy Spirit is working through the Bride of Christ that is still here in this world. 1 Thessalonians 2 speaks of the coming "day of the Lord," which really does not include the Rapture. Because of this, Paul references the Tribulation, then the Millennial Kingdom, and afterwards. Because of that, at least in that section of Scripture, the Rapture has already occurred.

In fact, it is patently clear that because this present world wants to push God away and wants no part of Him any longer, He will oblige them by not only removing the Church (a constant reminder of God, His Presence, and His authority over all of His Creation), but once the Church is gone, He will oblige the world by sending a *strong delusion* so that they will believe the lie.

> *"...and with all the deception of wickedness for those who perish, because they did not receive the love of the truth so as to be saved. For this reason God will send upon them a deluding influence so that they will believe what is false, in order that they all may be judged who did not believe the truth, but took pleasure in wickedness"* (2 Thessalonians 2:10-12).

Notice Paul's words carefully. God will send a delusion "*because [those who perish] did not receive the love of the truth so as to be saved.*"

The entire world will so desperately want to be "done" with God that He will remove the Church *and* will send them the deluding influence they ask for in order that they may fully embrace what is false. This is done so that they will be judged since they took no pleasure in truth, but in wickedness. I cannot stress how important it is for us to understand these facts.

The world will want God completely out of the picture. They will come to a point where they want nothing more than to not even *think* of God any longer. In order for this to occur in society the true Church will need to be removed. What a *tragedy*!

Today, if people will not harden their hearts, God will show them the truth of salvation. Many who see that truth do embrace it and become children of God.

But here's the problem. At some point in the future, because the world will no longer have any love for the truth about God and will wish for nothing more than to believe that He does not exist, God will grant their wish. In so doing so, though, these people who desperately want no more reminders about God will become God's enemies.

People today who are not saved still have some measure of protection from God. He still loves and cares for them. He still reaches out to them. He still yearns for them to come to know Him and see Him as the loving God He is, but because there will be a time of absolute and abject refusal to acknowledge God, the people then will literally be pushed away *from* God, *by* God. The delusion that He sends will – for most of them – give them the relief for which they long. The only problem with that is that they will then be *treated* as enemies of God.

I don't think people – even Christians (myself included) – understand the full ramifications of such a situation. The future will be more than bleak. After the true Church is raptured and God sends His deluding influence, the people living during that time will experience a completely abysmal time on this planet. Though we know from Scripture that people will still receive His salvation, it will be under the harshest terms one can imagine.

We think we have it bad now in the world? It pales in comparison to what life will be like in the future after the Church is raptured and the deluding influence is sent by God. The aftermath of both events (Rapture and delusion) will be so devastating and pervasive throughout global society that people will actually wish for death because they believe that at least the horrors of this life will be over (cf. Revelation 6). Of course, those who think that way have no understanding of who God is and the fact that He is everywhere at once. To die from this life means to lose every opportunity to see the truth regarding salvation.

Following the Rapture, the level of evil that will already exist at that point in the world will rise *dramatically* since the "restrainer" (aka the restraining influence of the Holy Spirit through the true Church) will be greatly reduced. Think of a dam that gives way of its own accord. The water it held back rushes into the area that was in front of the dam, the area that the dam actually *protected* from flooding.

As the Holy Spirit moves aside (because of the Rapture of the Church), the evil that will have been held in check up to that point will rush into the world creating a level of apostasy that will have been never realized before, even during Noah's day (cf. Matthew 24).

> *"It seems that Paul was referring here to the departure from the Christian faith of professing (not genuine) Christians, soon after the Rapture, at the beginning of 'the day of the Lord.' This was not the same 'apostasy' that he and*

> *other apostles wrote and spoke of elsewhere, when they*
> *warned of departure from the faith before the Rapture (1*
> *Tim. 4:1-3; 2 Tim. 4:3-4; James 5:1-8; 2 Pet. 2; 3:3-6;*
> *Jude).*"[11]

Logically, if the Rapture *does* occur prior to the Tribulation period, only authentic Christians will be caught up to the Lord in the heavenly realms. Those people remaining on earth will be the lost (atheists, agnostics, those of false religions, etc.) and those who only *thought* themselves to be actual Christians, but in point of fact, were not.

The world will literally tremble at the way society has been left following the Rapture. Imagine the true shock and awe that will envelop people in abject fear. Imagine how you would react to the fact that millions of people who once inhabited this planet are no longer here, all of them gone in less than an instant. This event will have terrible repercussions for all of society and the earth itself. This is not merely because of the coming Tribulation, but because of the dramatic increase in unleashed and unchecked evil that will fill the void left by the removal of millions of true Christians!

The Rapture is *not* simply an event that affects true Christians here on earth (and those Christians who have previously died). This one event will cause cataclysmic changes in society itself with fear and dread turning to greater depths of apostasy for most individuals.

Once this "departure" of true Christians occurs, the world will be much better positioned to accept the man of sin/man of lawlessness to whom Paul refers in 2 Thessalonians 2. It is difficult to appreciate the level of apostasy that is going to occur and has, in fact, begun. But obviously, the Rapture will occur at a point in which society cannot go back. God will see their resolute desire to go forward, embracing

---

[11] http://soniclight.com/constable/notes/pdf/2thessalonians.pdf, p. 14

Holy Spirit Restrains Full Measure of Evil through the True (Invisible) Church in Society

Dam holds back water from flooding town below and also used as resevoir to provide water for drinking, irrigation, bathing, etc.

Dam now holds no water back, which floods town, destroying crops, homes, and people.

Two Sides of the Rapture

1 True Church Meets the Lord in the Air!

2 Chaos, havoc, dramatic increase in evil on earth!

evil that much more, and He will give society what it wants while protecting His Bride, the Church.

We are living in a time when it has become an accepted norm to hate and speak out against Christians, against the one, true God, against the morality that He demands, and against the truth He *is*. People don't want to hear about the Christian God, though they can and do put up with the Islamic god, or other gods. Some, of course, are opposed to any and all gods in society. The prejudice and vehemence against God and Christianity (and even Judaism itself since from Israel came Jesus, the Messiah) has become palpable and vindictive. It's as though the gauntlet has been thrown down and direct attacks are now the norm.

It is as though this anti-God movement (as one writer calls it) is now center stage, dragging society with it in all attempts to separate itself from God.

> *"This worldwide anti-God movement will be so universal as to earn for itself a special designation: 'the apostasy'— i.e., the climax of the increasing apostate tendencies evident before the rapture of the church."*[12]

This is becoming all the more evident in all areas of society. Try to imagine what society will look like *after* the Rapture occurs and the Holy Spirit is no longer working *through* the true Church to restrain

---

[12] http://soniclight.com/constable/notes/pdf/2thessalonians.pdf, p. 15

that evil and call the lost of this world to Him. Is it any wonder that men's hearts will fail them out of fear, as we learn in Luke 21:26 where Jesus is teaching about the end times and the final seven-year period leading up to His physical return to this planet?

Think of what Jesus said in Matthew 24:12. "*Because lawlessness is increased, most people's love will grow cold.*" That love exists today is due only to the fact that the true Church is still in this world, allowing God's love toward the unsaved in society to be evident. However, with the true Church taken out of the world, any semblance of love toward our neighbors and the lost souls of this world is also gone. This is a terrible thought to consider, something that the unsaved of this world certainly do not think about.

The apostasy throughout the globe now is due to the world's rejection of God. Apostasy is ultimately rejecting God's rule. Whether it's done by professing Christians, backsliding Christians, or the lost people of this world, it all boils down to apostasy. Apostasy creates lawlessness.

One example of this is the New Age movement, which became well-known during the 1970s and 80s (and was/is an outgrowth of the earlier movement of Theosophy with leaders like Madame Blavatsky and Alice Bailey) and has become far more acceptable in society now as truth. New Age proponents teach principles that are completely opposed to Judeo-Christian principles found in God's Word. This is even being done *inside* churches and institutions today that heretofore have long been bastions of biblical truth since their inception but now are moving away from those tenets to embrace everything New Age as they move forward.

In New Age religion, in an effort to completely remove the only true God from all of society, people have begun chasing after ideologies and principles in which they are taught that they themselves are the god they seek and should worship. They need not look beyond themselves, but merely within. This is New Age-ism in a nutshell. This is the same lie that Satan used in the Garden of Eden.

But according to Paul, it won't be until *after* the Tribulation begins that the Antichrist will be revealed to the world. Paul tells us that eventually, this man of lawlessness (who will head the *system* of lawlessness) will waltz into the Holy of Holies and declare himself to be God. While some take Paul's reference to this in 2 Thessalonians 2 metaphorically, it seems clear that Paul is referring to a literal event, like the one that became known as the "abomination of desolation" spoken of by Jesus in Matthew 24. Jesus was referring to Antiochus Epiphanes defiling the Temple in 168 BC by slaughtering a pig on the altar and sprinkling the blood inside the Holy of Holies.

But again, for the most part, all of 2 Thessalonians is Paul's attempt to correct an error that had been cause for concern to believers in Thessalonica. The issue we are dealing with in 2 Thessalonians 2:1-12 is whether or not the "day of the Lord" had begun in Paul's time. The believers to whom Paul wrote were understandably unnerved because apparently some letter or messenger had come to them alleging to be from Paul, saying that the "day of the Lord" (starting with the Tribulation) had already commenced. Paul took pen to paper to assure those believers that no such message had come from him. He also took the time to *remind* them of the things he had already taught them, including the Rapture and the "day of the Lord" events.

We know from 2 Thessalonians that those believers were, in fact, experiencing tremendous persecution. They naturally wanted to know if they had somehow misunderstood what Paul had taught them and whether the Tribulation had actually begun.

Paul responds with careful wording and a heart filled with love for them. No, the "day of the Lord" had not begun yet (v. 2). He explains *why* it hadn't happened yet. Paul tells them that no one should deceive them into thinking that the Tribulation had begun and he reminds them that several things needed to occur before it could begin. If we take 1 Thessalonians together with 2 Thessalonians, it is also clear that the Rapture would have to happen before the Tribulation could begin.

There would need to be a "falling away" first. After this falling away, which would lead up to, and in some ways allow, the "day of the Lord," the "man of sin/son of perdition" would be revealed. He will be revealed because he will be the only individual who will actually be able to bring any sort of peace to the Middle East (Daniel 9:27). He will "*confirm a covenant with the many for one week.*" This cannot occur until the falling away happens first. In essence, the confirmation of a covenant with the many (Israel's leaders) is the actual event that kicks off the "day of the Lord," which begins with the Tribulation, then carries through to the Second Coming, judgment of the nations, Millennial Kingdom, and then the Great White Throne Judgment.

Also, Paul seems to reiterate in 2 Thessalonians 2:6-7 the concept of the Rapture.

> *"And you know what restrains him now, so that in his time he will be revealed. For the mystery of lawlessness is already at work; only he who now restrains will do so until he is taken out of the way."*

In 1 Thessalonians 4, Paul explains the details of the Rapture, how the invisible Church (both living and dead) will be the beneficiary of it, and how God directs it. Here, in the above passage, Paul seems to be emphasizing the "down" side of the Rapture for those people left on earth afterwards. He's pointing out how things will turn terribly ugly because of the fact that the growing apostasy will be allowed to grow tremendously since the Holy Spirit will no longer have the Church to work through in saving grace. This seems to be the logical understanding of the passage here with Paul noting the terrible effects the aftermath of the Rapture will have on this earth.

In spite of this, some interpret these passages to teach a Rapture occurring at the end of the Tribulation, during the event in which Jesus returns to the earth. That seems like an odd interpretation given the way Paul speaks about the Rapture and the Tribulation itself.

Regarding the return of our Lord, Dr. Thomas Constable notes the following:

> *"[N]evertheless, the view of a posttribulational rapture is impossible for the simple reason that it makes meaningless the very argument that Paul was presenting in the Thessalonian letters. Paul was arguing for the imminence of Christ's return. This is to be the major source of comfort for suffering believers. If Christ will not come until after the great tribulation (that is, a special period of unusual and intense suffering still in the future), then the return of the Lord is not imminent and tribulation rather than deliverance is what we must anticipate."*[13]

Things *are* moving toward the final seven years of man-led human history. Globalists (Technocrats) are using a system by which they believe they will control the entire globe. It certainly appears from numerous places in Scripture that God will allow them to reach their goals. While it sounds like something out of a sci-fi movie, the reality is that they are well on their way to completing it. Based on what we have discussed, it certainly appears that this world can only move so far toward a system completely enveloped in lawlessness while the Church remains. In order for the mystery of lawlessness that Paul speaks of to go full tilt, the Rapture is required before that can occur.

---

[13] http://soniclight.com/constable/notes/pdf/1thessalonians.pdf

Authentic Christians – God's moral compass in this world – empowered by the presence of the Holy Spirit keep evil in check. Without true Christians here, the world would fall completely to satanic evil. Just as God judged the entire world during the days of Noah (yet kept Noah and his family completely away from His judgment), and as God rained down judgment on Sodom and Gomorrah during the days of Lot (but directed Lot and family away from that area so that they would not be harmed by God's judgment), this world will face the full force of God's judgment once the true Church is gone from this world.

The world increasingly wants nothing to do with God. What they fail to realize is that though they do not accept Him, He offers a measure of His protection (He sends the rain on the just and unjust, etc.) because of the presence of His Church in this world. The world doesn't see it that way. Instead, they do everything they can to throw off the "fetters" they believe exist (mainly through conscience) and want no reminders of Him at all (cf. Psalm 2).

God will grant them this, but first He will remove the Bride of Christ before He begins dealing in abject judgment with the earth populated by people who hate Him. What the world fails to see is that by rejecting God (and Him giving them over to themselves; cf. Romans 1), they are rejecting *everything* about God including His love, compassion, and salvation. This is the danger. Rejecting God like this means inviting His wrath. It is that simple.

Chapter 5

Apostasy Leads to the Tribulation

W e spoke of the increasing lawlessness (mystery of lawlessness) that Paul speaks of in 2 Thessalonians 2 and how the Rapture occurring *prior* to the Tribulation will allow and enable the lawlessness that will exist in society at that point to increase dramatically. Since the true Church will be pulled off this earth in preparation for a time of global wrath from God poured out via three sets of seven judgments (or twenty-one total: Seven Seals, Seven Trumpets, Seven Bowls), the Holy Spirit will no longer have the Church to use as a means of keeping evil in check.

The resultant vacuum created by the Rapture will quickly fill in with a major jump in lawlessness. Evil will nearly have complete and unchecked sway over all the earth. I say "nearly" because the Holy Spirit will still be here (as God is always everywhere) opening the eyes of the blind, helping them to see that salvation in Jesus is the only way. One of the known ways He will do this is through the 144,000 Jewish evangelists He saves and seals for the task.

Because of the Church's presence in the world, evil can only do so much. Yes, it is growing as Scripture tells us it will, but it cannot be as bad as evil would like it to be while the Holy Spirit (via the Church) is in the way. His influence in the world must be reduced, at least for a time, to allow lawlessness to gain such a foothold over the entirety of the earth that there is nothing left but for God to begin pouring out His judgment.

In 1 Thessalonians 4, starting with verse 13, Paul begins to provide information about the Rapture. Again, the word "rapture" is from the Latin *rapturo*, which translated to English is "Rapture" ("caught up"). As Paul clearly notes, he explains this because of direct revelation he received from the Lord (cf. v. 15). Paul was given information that had either previously been unknown or the meaning was unknown. The meaning of these "mysteries" were given to Paul to share with believers during his time and ultimately during ours as well.

Let's focus on verses 13 and 14 of 1 Thessalonians 4:

> "*But we do not want you to be uninformed, brethren, about those who are asleep, so that <u>you will not grieve as do the rest who have no hope</u>. For if we believe that Jesus died and rose again, even so God will bring with Him those who have fallen asleep in Jesus.*" (emphasis added)

I've emphasized a portion of the text because I would like to bring out a point that clarifies things regarding the Thessalonian believers and why Paul was not referring to any other form of Rapture except a PreTrib Rapture (one that occurs before the Tribulation). Please note that the main reason Paul is offering insight to the Thessalonians is so that they will not grieve as the world grieves when someone who does not know Jesus dies. Paul wants them to be informed about what will eventually be happening. As we learn in 2 Thessalonians 2, Paul is teaching and correcting their problematic understanding of future events related to the Rapture, the Tribulation, and the Second Coming itself.

The Thessalonian believers were upset because several of the believers there had already died. The Thessalonians who remained alive were grieving for them, but not because they had died. They were grieving because they mistakenly believed that these folks had missed something. What did they miss? Was it A) The Rapture, B) the Tribulation, or C) the Second Coming?

It appears that they were upset thinking the dead believers had missed the Rapture. We can clearly see this in verses 15 through 18.

> *"For this we say to you by the word of the Lord, that we who are alive and remain until the coming of the Lord, will not precede those who have fallen asleep. For the Lord Himself will descend from heaven with a shout, with the voice of the archangel and with the trumpet of God, and the dead in Christ will rise first. Then we who are alive and remain will be caught up together with them in the clouds to meet the Lord in the air, and so we shall always be with the Lord. Therefore comfort one another with these words."*

Let's consider something. First, why would the Thessalonian believers be grieving for people who would be **missing** the Tribulation? Can you imagine it? *"Oh Paul, we are so saddened that some believers in our church have now died and will miss the horrors of the Tribula-*

tion!" That is so absurd, it's difficult to believe that there are people who believe that is what they were concerned about. Second, why would these same living believers be upset if they believed the dead believers had missed the Rapture if it doesn't occur until the end of the Tribulation? Another absurdity.

It seems what the Thessalonian believers were upset about is that the dead believers may have missed the Rapture itself. That much seems clear based on the above verses (15-18). But if the Rapture doesn't happen until the end of the Tribulation as some believe, were the Thessalonian believers actually grieving over the fact that the dead believers had already died and wouldn't be part of the tremendous suffering of the Tribulation before they were raptured?

I know there are people today who are constantly complaining about PreTribbers and the alleged fact that we shrink from any type of persecution (as though wishing for the Rapture would make it so). In my view, their protestations simply point to their own twisted arrogance in thinking that they are the true and confirmed Christians because they are willing (or think they are) to suffer for Christ in any possible way imaginable and PreTribbers aren't. This is another absurdity, but it is difficult to discuss this with someone who holds such a high opinion of himself while denigrating other brothers and sisters whom he perceives to be cowards.

As mentioned earlier, the Thessalonian believers were grieving because they were concerned that those believers who had recently died would miss the Rapture. The message had come to them that the "day of the Lord" had already begun (cf. 2 Thessalonians 2:1ff). This would mean that the Rapture had already taken place since it was to occur before the Tribulation. Paul wrote to clarify to them that neither event had occurred yet, but when the Rapture did occur, those who had died in Christ would go to heaven just before those who were alive.

Also in the 2 Thessalonians 2 passage, Paul explains the logical order of events, and even though he does not specifically mention the Rapture by name there, he alludes to it by listing the events that would lead up to and occur inside the Tribulation. He explains that a great falling away (apostasy) would need to occur first that would open the door for the coming "man of sin" to ultimately be revealed to the world.

When the Rapture does occur, those who are dead "in Christ" (this does _not_ include Old Testament saints), then those alive will be caught up to meet with the Lord in the air.

It is clear from the above text that we meet the Lord in the air and in the clouds. Some then assume that Jesus continues His trek to the earth with those who have been caught up to meet Him in the air. If so, then this is the end of the Tribulation when He comes back to earth and sets up His Millennial Kingdom. This would make the Rapture coincide with His Second Coming, and there are numerous problems with that view.

In commenting on 1 Thessalonians 4:18 and the problem related to a PostTrib Rapture, Dr. Thomas Constable notes the following:

> *"...the view of a posttribulational rapture is impossible for the simple reason that it makes meaningless the very argument that Paul was presenting in the Thessalonian letters. Paul was arguing for the imminence of Christ's return. This is to be the major source of comfort for suffering believers. If Christ will not come until after the great tribulation (that is, a special period of unusual and intense suffering still in the future), then the return of the*

*Lord is not imminent and tribulation rather than deliver-
ance is what we must anticipate."[14]*

There is great misunderstanding related to the concept of "imminence" today. It does not mean "soon," but actually means "at any
moment." PostTribbers believe there are any number of things that
must occur prior to the Lord's physical return. Unfortunately, if this
is true, then Paul has no clue as to the actual meaning of "imminence"
and he is giving the Thessalonian believers false hope.

In reality, "imminence" means that Jesus is standing on the other side
of the door and could walk through it at any moment. Obviously, God
alone knows the exact time when He will do so to call His Bride up to
meet Him. We do not, and because of that, it appears to us as an "at
any moment" situation. We also need to understand that God is outside time and therefore not constrained by it. The only time He is so
constrained is when He voluntarily comes into our dimension as Jesus did. Currently, though God is omnipresent, He operates from outside our sphere of time, yet sees everything at once.

The Rapture of the Church is imminent and therefore *could* happen at
any moment. There is nothing – that we know of – that keeps Him
from calling us up to Him right now except His own timing, to which
we are not privy.

To wrap this up, Paul was doing his level best to comfort the Thessalonian believers by eradicating the error that was seeking to infil-
trate that local body. He was setting the record straight by telling
them what was what regarding the Rapture and the start of the Tribulation.

In Matthew 24:21, Jesus tells us that whatever has come before by
way of distress, tribulation, madness, violence, and lawlessness will

---

[14] http://www.soniclight.com/constable/notes/pdf/1thessalonians.pdf, pp 38-39
(2/18/2015)

not be as great as what this world will experience during the Tribulation period. If we can imagine Satan and his minions being given nearly free rein throughout the globe, we will have some idea of what Jesus is referring to here.

But the world cannot get to that point as long as the Holy Spirit is working through the presence of the *invisible* Church. People are constantly complaining about the way the church is asleep or has failed. What they fail to see is that God's invisible Church, Christ's Bride, is fine. He is the Author and Perfecter of our faith and will finish what He began. He will bring His purposes to fruition in and through the *invisible* Church.

The only "church" that is asleep at the wheel is the *visible* church, filled with false teachers. That "church" has nothing to do with Christ's Bride and people need to be aware of that huge difference.

It is the *visible* church – or all of Christendom made up of professing Christians and even atheists – that is anti-God and will fall away from any semblance of godly morality and biblical beliefs.

Our job – as true Christians – is not to change the *invisible* Church or America (we can't). Our job is to fulfill the Great Commission. Take no thought about tomorrow because there is enough evil in this current day. Focus on spreading the gospel, preaching to the lost, and inviting people to come to know Jesus Christ, the only One who can save them from sin and eternal death.

In the meantime, look up and understand that things are moving according to God's pace and program, regardless of how things look. He is not unable. He is not asleep. He is not uncaring. His purposes – all of them – will be fulfilled as they are being fulfilled. You don't have to concern yourself with that. You only have to concern yourself with being a solid witness – in word and deed – regarding the saving grace of Jesus Christ, who gave Himself for us that we might live. This good news needs to be spread far and wide, while there is time and while it is still day.

Chapter 6

Full Force of Globalism

C ertainly, the Rapture will pave the way for globalists to push their system to the limit and out into the open. Not only would they likely have little to no resistance from the remainder of humanity to whatever they have designed for society, but most of society will be completely receptive.

We need to remember that once the Rapture happens, there is a plus side as well as a negative side. The plus side is that millions of true Christians will meet their Lord and Savior in the air to be with Him forever! The negative side is the aftermath of the Rapture on the earth. It's not just people being "left behind," so to speak.

The Rapture will allow for an environment conducive to creating the necessary dramatic societal shift. It will seem as though the gates of hell have been thrown open wide. Who can truly imagine this type of evil permeating all areas of society? Even though the apostle John does his best to tell us what he saw, we still cannot fully grasp the terrible things that will occur on the earth once the true Church is gone, and with it the influencing character of the Holy Spirit that dwelt within each Christian.

We need to realize that after the Rapture, evil will overwhelm society. It will create tremendous fear in people. They will want anything that will give them some peace of mind.

The Rapture is the indirect catalyst that certainly helps the global system currently being constructed to come to completion. This, in turn, leads ultimately to the start of the Tribulation. It will do so in part because of the utter economic disaster that confronts the world due to the results of the Rapture. This one event will help to cause/create cataclysmic changes throughout the world's economies that will take years to fully measure and repair.

In fact, a best case scenario would be for the entire world to do a "start over" in which everything begins again with globalists and their experts (scientists, engineers, etc.) ready to rebuild the system better than before, while further enslaving all people of all nations. The tragedy here is that for a measure of security and sense of peace, by and large, the people of the world will go along with what the Technocracy demands. People will want to feel some measure of safety again so they will succumb to the demands of leaders who will promise them security, but make them virtual prisoners. At the start, the relinquishment of freedom is accepted. Unfortunately, as people become Christians, due to the evangelizing efforts of the 144,000 (cf. Revelation 7), things will become literally measured in life and death. This will also be true as things progress up to and include taking the

Technocracy to Tribulation

mark of the beast (cf. Revelation 13). People will begin to see the hell that Technocracy has been allowed to create.

But, if God has taken the time to place within His Word information concerning the event that kicks off the Tribulation, then it should go without saying that knowing it is exceedingly important. However, let's be clear again that knowing that event does **not** also mean that we will know *when* that event will occur. We will simply recognize it when it *does* occur.

We know ahead of time the exact event that will start the ball rolling where the Tribulation is concerned. Yet, as Christians, this should not be our focus. Our focus should be on the return of Jesus. I have no idea when I will die, but I know I will die one day. Paul says that to be absent in the body is to be present with the Lord (2 Corinthians 5:8). If that is true – and it is – should I not live my life knowing that at any moment, I may be taking my last breath? If anything helps us to know what is important in this life, it is knowing that death is always but one breath away.

As noted, God's plan (including the coming Tribulation) deals with humanity's continued rejection of God. Paul has made it very clear as to just how bad mankind will become in these latter days, the days leading up to and including the Tribulation period.

> *"This know also, that in the last days perilous times shall come. For men shall be lovers of their own selves, covetous, boasters, proud, blasphemers, disobedient to parents, un-thankful, unholy, Without natural affection, trucebreakers, false accusers, incontinent, fierce, despisers of those that are good, Traitors, heady, highminded, lovers of pleasures more than lovers of God...Having a form of godliness, but denying the power thereof: from such turn away"* (2 Timo-thy 3:1-5).

What an indictment. Paul lays it out very clearly for us. He doesn't mince words. People will simply become more evil as the time approaches the beginning of the Tribulation period.

We see this selfishness evident as we move toward that day, as many believe the government owes them something. They're not willing to work for anything. Too many have no qualms about taking what is not theirs, attacking people who have done nothing to them, and in general, doing whatever seems right to them in their own eyes. This is the how people of today live, as their own gods, deciding what is right and what is wrong. They answer only to themselves. We can see that we are nearing that day of which Paul speaks.

It is difficult to wrap our brains around all that will be included in the Tribulation, but God has presented us with information concerning this period of time and it is best we delve into it to find some type of chronological order.

It is best to start with Daniel, but please note that we will be jumping around to include various passages from Scripture. The passage that we are going to deal with in Daniel is the only passage that provides insight into the full 70 "weeks," or 490 years, in which Israel will be trampled by Gentile nations, something that began with Babylon.

I believe we are currently *between* the 69th and 70th weeks of prophecy illuminated to Daniel. I'll show why shortly. I also believe that the 70th week (or the final seven years of human-led history) begins with one specific event. This event will begin those seven final years, years referred to as the Tribulation/Great Tribulation.

It is also very important to realize that unlike what others taught decades ago, the event that is to begin the Tribulation is *not* the Rapture. Though I *do* believe the Rapture occurs prior to the Tribulation as noted, the Rapture does not even enter into the Tribulation picture as far as we are concerned.

Simply understand that our perspective assumes the Rapture has already taken place. It is not connected to the Tribulation in any way, and because of that, the Tribulation could happen at any time *after* the Rapture occurs. In that sense then, while there might be an indirect connection, there is no direct connection. The Rapture could happen months or years prior to the beginning of the Tribulation.

However, I do not believe that the Tribulation can begin until *after* the Rapture occurs. There is still a specific event that *does* signal the beginning of the Tribulation. In order for this one event to occur, the nations will need to be ruled by a one-world government. That will require a common merchant system, which is currently being built by globalists and unseen by the average individual.

Patrick M. Wood speaks of several systems and devices in his book *Technocracy Rising* that we know are there, but don't even really consider anymore because we've gotten so used to them. These include surveillance systems. Many are already found in your home, your car, and your neighborhood.

The average person has no real clue about these things, and if or when someone *does* discuss these subjects as harmful in that they rob us of our privacy, that person is easily written off as a "conspiracy theorist," with all the attendant negative connotations that go with that label. Few like to be labeled as such and usually learn to avoid discussing those things, except among others who also believe there is a certain degree of truth in them.

Chapter 7

Today's "Forbin" Project

I n 1970, Universal Pictures released a movie called "Colossus: The Forbin Project." It was based on the sci-fi book published in 1966 simply titled *Colossus*, written by Dennis Feltham Jones.

The movie centers around the concept that two supercomputers – one from the US called Colossus and one from the USSR called Guardian – make contact with one another and essentially take over the world. They do so by basically holding the world hostage to their demands.

I recall watching the movie, and though I would undoubtedly think aspects of it were just plain silly in today's technological world, the concept of computers enslaving the entire human race is not science fiction, but something that one particular group we call globalists has been endeavoring to bring to fruition for some time now.

I fully realize that there are those who scoff at the idea that a cadre of individuals who want nothing more than to rule the world exists. But the truth of the matter is that I have a higher source than so-called conspiracy files. The Bible itself portrays a future which is controlled first by ten "kings" (cf. Revelation 17) and ultimately by one man. This man of sin/man of lawlessness (as Paul refers to him in 2 Thessalonians 2) will one day rule the entire world. That is not science fiction.

According to the Bible, this individual – also called Antichrist – will be fully empowered supernaturally to rule and control nearly all aspects of life on this planet. If people want to label the Antichrist and the coming new world order as a conspiracy theory, that's up to them. As far as I'm concerned, the Bible has a great track record, so I will continue to defer to it.

The idea that computers will control the future is not really far-fetched by today's standards. In fact, the term "Smart Grid" or "Energy Web" comes to mind when I think about how computers, Wi-Fi networks, and even home appliances are being made to work together to create a grid/network designed to control all energy usage. This is key.

Will computers control all of this? Yes, of course, but obviously they need to be programmed and are being programmed by the people who run things. No, it's not the government. Governments are used by globalists to bring their dreams of a totalitarian society to fruition so that they are the ones in control.

I know that many people today believe there was/is a difference between people like George W. Bush and Barack Obama. Bush, being on the "Right" – a conservative – is seen as more humane, more caring, more loyal, etc., by those who call themselves conservatives. On the other hand, Obama, on the "Left," is someone who is seen (and deliberately portrayed) as an individual who couldn't care less about America and has only its destruction in mind.

In other words, it's easy to love Bush and hate Obama if you're conservative. It's also true that if you're liberal, it's easy to hate Bush and love Obama. The problem, though, is that both of these men have done and do things that destroy the sovereignty of America, but not of their own accord.

Author Patrick M. Wood, in his book *Technocracy Rising*, points out something that Bush did that indicates his allegiance to the globalists. It's something you need to know about.

> *"The Office of Electricity Delivery and Energy Reliability was created in 2003 under President George W. Bush and was elevated in stature in 2007 by creating the position of Assistant Secretary of Electricity Delivery and Energy Reliability to head it.*
>
> *"It is not stated who 'charged' the Department of Energy Reliability to this task, but since the Secretary of Energy answers directly to the President as a cabinet position, it is self-evident that the directive came from the President, whether Bush or Obama. In any case, there was no Congressional legislation that required it, nor has there been any Congressional oversight controlling it."*[15]

So what's the problem? The problem is that once the position had been established by Bush, it needed funding, which happened almost immediately to some degree and in earnest on October 27, 2009, according to Wood.

---

[15] Patrick M. Wood, *Technocracy Rising* (2015), p. 142

> *"[T]he Obama administration unveiled its Smart Grid plan by awarding $3.4 billion to 100 Smart Grid projects. According to the Department of Energy's first press release, these awards were to result in the installation of [devices and sensors related to Smart Grid growth and operation]."*[16]

Your home may well have what is known as a gas/electric Digital Smart Meter (also called an Advanced Meter), which has the capacity to talk with the appliances in your home. How? By virtue of the fact that appliances being built today include a circuit board or smart chip that will "communicate" with your Smart Meter.

In essence, what is being created through the Smart Grid is a completely interconnected "Internet of Things"[17] in which access to your home via Wi-Fi, chips, circuit boards, and Digital Smart Meters is handed over to "regulators" who will then be in the position of controlling how much energy you use (because they will be able to track and control your usage; makes you wonder what else they will be able to track). This is done through *unique identifiers*.

This is all being done in the name of "climate change/global warming," and of course globalists, who don't want to be seen as the sneaky, money-grubbing elitists they are, want us to think that consumers will save money and that this so-called "Energy Web" (as Wood refers to it) will have major benefits extending even to third-world countries.

Digital Smart Meters (both gas and electric) have the capacity to track data and report it back to those who will collect it and make decisions based on that information. In this way, they will be able to monitor your use of energy and even shut down appliances that they believe use too much energy. Welcome to the Forbin Project at work.

---

[16] Patrick M. Wood, *Technocracy Rising* (2015), p. 142
[17] http://whatis.techtarget.com/definition/Internet-of-Things (04/14/2015)

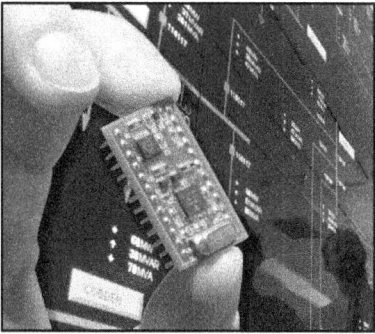

A government agency called Pacific Northwest National Laboratory (PNNL) has created a circuit board they call *"Grid Friendly Appliance Controller,"* and it will do just that.

Wood goes into a great amount of detail regarding the facts concerning the Smart Grid that is being built today.

The *Grid Friendly Appliance Controller* (shown at left) is small indeed.

Though the grid itself that is being built is *physical*, we cannot literally see it since it is part of a nationwide electrical framework. Very much like the electrical system that runs your home or car, it's certainly there, but it is part of the "inner workings" and is something we don't even think about unless a problem becomes associated with it.

We are aware, at least to some extent, of the way an electrical grid works, even if our expertise is not in that area. But because this system is being constructed that will literally tie our home (via Smart Meters) into this national framework, this *should* be cause for alarm. Since we don't think of it, however, and there is no physical structure (like the old Tower of Babel) that we can actually see and touch, most people aren't concerned.

Suffice it to say that in the near future, everything will have the *potential* to be tracked through the (ultimately) worldwide Smart Grid that is under construction. Controlling the energy we use via the appliances we have is a major aspect of control. We also already know about the tracking capabilities of the NSA in regards to our communication; in the same way our energy use will be tracked and controlled by others.

We need to understand that the future is here and a sophisticated computer matrix grid is being built out of sight, but under our very noses. Globalists want (and will have) control of all aspects of our lives, and while they claim to be concerned for third-world countries that cannot survive on their own, the reality is that globalists want control for themselves. Their alleged concern is all for show. They want to take charge of the limited resources they believe this planet has, which is why the talk of "sustainable development" is one of the bigger catch phrases today, along with "climate change."

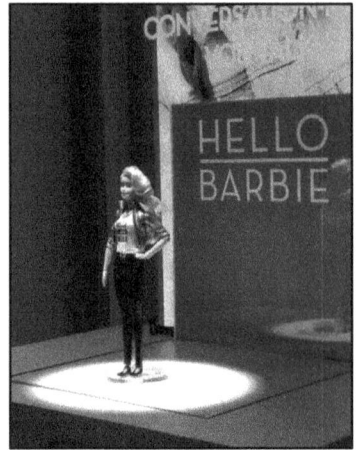

Globalists aren't the least bit interested in you or me. They're interested in stealing as much money as they possibly can from one government or the next to increase their wealth in order to wield power over the rest of us. Though they speak of saving money for the consumer, the only ones who will actually save money are the companies producing the energy, not the consumers.

Creating products with smart chips and "Grid Friendly Appliance Controller" boards in them costs money and we will be paying for them. It's not about us saving money. It's about globalists gaining and maintaining control over all aspects of our lives. This is the core belief of the Technocracy movement itself, as Wood explains in his book.

Every aspect of our lives will be tracked and controlled. Even toy companies are getting involved. Mattel's newest Barbie is called "Hello Barbie" (with a fall 2015 release date) and has the capability of having a "discussion" with the child who plays with it.

"Hello Barbie works by recording a child's voice with an embedded microphone that is triggered by pressing a button on the doll. As the doll 'listens,' audio recordings travel over the Web to a server where the snippets of speech are recognized and processed. That information is used to help form Hello Barbie's responses."[18]

Given the above information, privacy advocate groups are very concerned about this newest "toy" from Mattel. Some are even calling it "Eavesdropping Barbie." If you have Wi-Fi in your home (and the doll only works with Wi-Fi) and the doll is "on" and within earshot, then conceivably, Hello Barbie could "listen" in on your conversation, send it over your Wi-Fi network to Mattel where it is stored, and, via a very powerful algorithm, create a response to what the doll just "heard." Is there a reason to be concerned?

Groups like Campaign for a Commercial-Free Childhood are attempting to pressure Mattel to stop the project before it even goes into full production.

The fact that Hello Barbie relies so heavily on a Wi-Fi network connection is interesting. Like Smart Meters and smart appliances that connect us all to the under-construction Smart Grid, video games have been keeping kids hooked up to the Internet for a while now. It would not surprise me to learn that there are companies out there dedicated to learning everything they can about your child's involvement on the 'Net through video games, and now through toy dolls.

The truth is that globalists have been building their own version of the Forbin Project for a few generations now and they will follow it through to completion. Accordingly, it will be this same system that

---

[18] http://www.washingtonpost.com/blogs/the-switch/wp/2015/03/11/privacy-advocates-try-to-keep-creepy-eavesdropping-hello-barbie-from-hitting-shelves/?tid=sm_tw (3/17/2015)

the coming Antichrist uses to his own benefit after the globalists have done all the hard work of building it to gain control of the world's resources. It will be a match made in hell (globalists and Antichrist), one that will allow Antichrist to gain dominance and that globalists won't even see coming.

Wresting control from people is the reason globalists do everything, from promoting "climate change" to "gun control" to "same-sex unions" to "Islamophobia" to their war on Christianity and everything in between. They will do everything and anything to wrest oversight from we, the people. Though they argue that they are philanthropists, they are the furthest things from that. They want to control, and to control means to enslave.

For the record, if the Bible is correct, we cannot defeat globalists, certainly not on a national level. It's possible to push them back at the local level (and Wood says as much in his book's eleventh chapter), but even those victories may be short-lived.

I'm just telling you what the future looks like. Do your own research to learn whether or not what I'm telling you is fact or fiction. If fact, you'll then know where to put your energies.

Chapter 8

Increasing the Grid's Reach

The state of Oregon has decided to begin keeping track of how many miles each person in that state drives. What would be the purpose of such a move? Why, *taxation*, of course. Interestingly enough, this will be done by making vehicles noticeable on the grid by collecting mileage data. A built-in GPS device will also know when the car drives *out* of Oregon.

As you'll recall, Technocracy is a movement in which efforts are made by those who have power to control the world's resources. While it officially began in the 1930s in the US, the technology simply wasn't there to keep such close track or control of these resources. In fact, consumers didn't have access to computers for their homes until the late 1970s/early 1980s, leaving the desires of the Technocracy movement little more than pipe dreams. Now, we literally carry small computers with us wherever we go in our "smart phones." Most homes have several computer systems, including laptops, desktops, tablets, and notebooks. Wherever we go, someone could conceivably track us.

Of course, with computers gaining popularity over the years, coupled with the creation and implementation of the Internet, globalists began to realize that their dreams of absolute control were possible. It's interesting to note that the Internet was created by and for the military decades ago as a way for scientists working with the military to remain in contact without having to actually physically be in the same place. Decades later, we have taken the Internet for granted since the federal government allowed it to be used for personal and commercial use outside the confines of the military.

Again though, the goal of globalists who oversee the Technocracy that author Wood speaks of is to *control energy* usage, the resources as well as how and how quickly those resources are used. Right now, most of us pay road taxes at the gas pump every time we fill our cars up.

Soon, Oregonians will have the option of either paying an additional tax at the gas pump or 1 1/2 cents per mile driven, which will be measured by a device that is attached to their car. Orwellian? You bet. I can only imagine the way this device might be used (and abused) so that globalists will gain even more control of society through the expansion of their dreamed-of Technocracy.

From *Automotive News*:

> "*Automotive News reports the state [of Oregon] will offer two options to its motorists: pay at the pump, or pay a 1.5-*

cent rate per mile traversed. The latter will be conducted through a device that plugs into a vehicle's OBD port, then gathers mileage data to determine how much the motorist will pay in tax."[19]

Right now, the program — set to begin July 1, 2015 — will be implemented by the Oregon Department of Transportation in partnership with *Sanef ITS Technologies America* and *Intelligent Mechatronic Systems*, the latter supplying the previously mentioned OBD (on-board diagnostic) mileage reader.

Beginning July 1, 2015, the state of Oregon will tap 5,000 people to volunteer to place a device on their cars to determine how many miles they drive. From there, the powers that be in Oregon's Department of Transportation will determine if the volunteers will receive a refund or invoice based on actual miles driven. It is likely that eventually, *everyone* in Oregon will have a device installed in their cars. The program will likely be adopted by other state governments as well.

According to OPB.org,[20] these plug-in devices have GPS capability to know when the vehicle travels out of Oregon (and won't count those miles). One volunteer – who works for the government as a state transportation commissioner – has volunteered to have the device placed on her vehicle. She welcomes the idea that people will know where she drives and how many miles she tracks. It's a potential invasion of privacy that she is unconcerned about, which tells you the mentality that people have today regarding the fact that the government is encroaching on our personal lives as much as it is, and many to most seem undaunted. In essence, though, this is how our cars are

---

[19] http://www.autonews.com/article/20150306/OEM05/150309871/oregon-prepares-nations-first-per-mile-road-tax (3/13/2015)
[20] http://www.opb.org/news/article/n3-washington-oregon-consider-mileage-based-road-tax/ (3/13/2014)

going to become part of the Smart Grid that's under construction, through mileage-counting devices accessible via GPS.

Interestingly enough, this additional 1 1/2 cents-per-mile-driven tax (via tracking devices on cars) is being instituted because of the *increased mileage* that electric cars (and Flex fuel vehicles) get on the road. Because of that, tax revenues have gone *down*. Since these high-end cars don't have to refill as often (or at all in the case of a fully electric vehicle), the amount of revenue taken in by Oregon via taxation at the pump has been reduced. Frankly, it's surprising that California was not the first to set up a system like this, but there's still time for that to happen, as it is doubtful that Oregon will be the only state introducing this new form of taxation via tracking.

Globalists have now figured out a way to take in just as much tax revenue from consumers who have purchased more expensive fuel-efficient cars as they did before. Let's remember, the reason consumers bought these cars was because we were told it would "save" money at the pump as well as be something that was more "efficient" for the world's "sustainable" development by reducing the "carbon footprint." In the end, the increased purchase price for their cars (for the privilege of not filling up as often) will possibly be zeroed out by having to pay a "tax per mile driven" anyway.

While globalists do their best to sell us things like "sustainable development," "energy efficiency," and "high mileage" in order to reduce our "carbon footprint" and save money at the same time, it really means nothing when we see how these things actually work out. Buying a more expensive fuel-efficient car to get higher mileage will, in this case, still likely cost consumers the same or more than having a car that gets lower mileage per gallon (requiring more fill-ups at the pump). Of course, people who still own those lower-mileage cars will wind up paying even more once this new tax is completely uploaded into Oregon's economy. In the end, buying a more "efficient" vehicle doesn't really pan out for the consumer, does it?

We need to remember that all of these seeming "individual" losses of freedom add up to a tremendous reduction in personal liberty of people throughout America. Whether it has to do with ensuring that the keepers of the Smart Grid can keep an eye on all your appliances, regulating them so that they use as little energy as possible, or attempting to force each person to drive fewer miles through a method of taxation determined through a small device placed on vehicles, the end result is that consumers will pay dearly for perceived *overuse* of energy.

The grid that is being built – including devices in home appliances and automobiles – is being constructed in order for globalists to gain and keep control of the population 24/7. Once the grid is fully established and humming along 24 hours per day, 365 days per year, these same globalists will be in the enviable position of being able to enslave us through coercive efforts using "energy" as the bait.

Of course, Satan simply wants a global system in place, which will make things infinitely easier for him to rule the world through Antichrist. He doesn't care about the energy usage. That is merely the carrot he dangles in front of globalists in order to get them to do his bidding. Because they believe the resources of earth are limited (and they are to an extent), they then believe they must reduce the population and take strong measures to control absolutely the amount of energy, along with the type of energy, that is being used at any one time.

Even now, the Environmental Protection Agency (EPA) is eyeing backyard barbecues. "*The agency announced that it is funding a University of California project to limit emissions resulting in grease drippings with a special tray to catch them and a 'catalytic' filtration system.*"[21] California has enough problems with a severe drought con-

---

[21] http://www.redflagnews.com/headlines-2015/backyard-burger-and-wiener-roasts-targeted-by-epa (3/18/2015)

tinuing in which experts are saying that within a year, California's water supply will be dried up, and California's leaders do not have a contingency plan for the state, either. In spite of this and other dramatic problems facing the state, Californians may also be forced to upgrade their grills (or buy new ones) that meet EPA guidelines. We are expected to believe that backyard barbecues are a major source of grease "pollution." In reality, this is simply another means that the government and its agencies are using to force more regulations on the people of America.

In response to this potential overreach by the government, lawmakers in Missouri are telling the EPA to back off. State Senator Eric Schmitt (R) from St. Louis stated the following:

> *"The idea that the EPA wants to find their way into our back yards, where we're congregating with our neighbors, having a good time, on the 4th of July, barbecuing pork steak or hamburgers, is ridiculous and it's emblematic of agency that's sort of out of control..."*[22]

In reality, agencies like the EPA are not "out of control," as Sen. Schmitt believes. They are doing exactly what they are tasked with doing. Their goal is to implement increasing regulations set forth by globalists who will not stop until they control every aspect of society.

Globalists are so fixated on building their grid to control energy uses and resources behind them that they have absolutely no clue that Satan is merely using them to create a system that he will one day completely take over and use to his advantage. We will get into this later in this book. For now, it is important to understand how globalists think and, based on how they think, what they are doing to ensure that they – and they alone – rule over the rest of society. Though they talk of fairness to all people, redistribution of wealth, and the elimi-

---

[22] http://www.foxnews.com/leisure/2015/03/17/lawmaker-calls-for-rebellion-against-epa-pollution-emissions-for-backyard/ (3/19/2015)

nation of wars, none of that really means anything in relation to their true goals.

From the same article, the University of California has noted "*that the technology they will study with the EPA grant is intended to reduce air pollution and cut the health hazards to BBQ 'pit masters' from propane-fueled cookers.*" The grant is in the sum of $15,000. Propane is one of the cleanest forms of energy around, but the EPA doesn't care. It only cares about putting more regulations in place. A world run by Technocrats means a world controlled by regulations. Again, globalists need to be in command of all aspects of society.

The overreach now includes attempts to control rainwater. More states are outlawing the ability of the homeowner to catch the water that falls out of the sky to be used later![23]

Globalists are blind to Satan's true purpose in using them. While they actually believe they are here to rule the world, in reality, Satan is using them to build the system of control, put it into place, and then once everything is set to go, he will step in and, through Antichrist, wrest control of the globalists' system of control from them for his own purposes.

In spite of this, it is clear that today's national leaders have no real clue that this is what's actually occurring in society, as we'll see in our next chapter. They play this great game of chess that appears to much of the world like true saber rattling. In reality, much of it is theater, in order to keep the average person constantly concerned about the unrest in the world.

---

[23] http://worldtruth.tv/collecting-rainwater-now-illegal-in-many-states-as-big-government-claims-ownership-over-our-water/ (3/18/2015)

Chapter 9

Duplicity of World Leaders

I t is not just a huge, complex, computer-controlled matrix, electronic "smart" grid, or what some have termed "Energy Web" that's being created behind the scenes. Actions of world leaders are also helping to create a system that not only caters to globalists, but proves they are in command.

Actions taken by elected officials are enough to make you scratch your head in confusion. We wonder if it's just us, or if they are too inane to realize we see their duplicity and hypocrisy. In reality, though, these people are not stupid, and that includes people like President Obama. He's not a stupid man by any stretch. He *confuses* the average person with his bold-faced lies because the average person doesn't realize for whom Mr. Obama actually works. While he is the president of the United States with his desk in the Oval Office, it almost appears as though he does not have the interests of the United States in mind. It's as though he *wants* America to fail. I believe this is due to the fact that though President Obama is *paid* by the American taxpayer (as are all elected officials), he actually works for *globalists*.

In essence, these people got him elected and then re-elected. They have an agenda and Mr. Obama is their willing puppet to make it happen. Anyone who would willingly place himself in that position is either extremely naïve, has no loyalties to any particular country, thinks essentially only of himself, or is a combination of the three.

In Mr. Obama's case, it is likely a combination of the second and third options. He probably does not care what happens to America because his loyalty is to the globalists who put him into office as president. Because of his own narcissistic tendencies, he tends not to see anything beyond his very small circle of relevance.

Reading through an article from Reuters about Venezuela recently initially gave me the impression of reading a "spoof" article because of the number of ironic quotes attributed to President Obama. He had chosen to place sanctions on certain high-ranking Venezuelan officials due to the alleged corruption of government there.

From Reuters: "*The United States on March 9, 2015 declared Venezuela a national security threat and ordered sanctions against seven officials from the oil-rich country in the worst bilateral diplomatic dispute since socialist President Nicolas Maduro took office in 2013.*"[24]

---

[24] http://www.reuters.com/article/2015/03/09/us-usa-venezuela-idUSKBN0M51NS20150309 (03/13/205)

The article goes on to state: *"U.S. President Barack Obama issued and signed the executive order, which senior administration officials said did not target Venezuela's energy sector or broader economy. But the move stokes tensions between Washington and Caracas just as U.S. relations with Cuba, a longtime U.S. foe in Latin America and key ally to Venezuela, are set to be normalized."*[25]

This is the part that begins to bring us to the point. We've been highlighting globalists and what Patrick M. Wood has called the Technocracy taking shape in this world. After what had been a bit of a rough ride with US-Venezuelan relations, with the latter breaking off diplomatic relations with the US in 2008, relations with Venezuela were once again established under President Obama in 2009. Prior to Obama, there were allegations of covert activity committed by US individuals whom Venezuela believed were trying to undermine and overthrow the nation.

Since Obama has taken office, words of praise *and* ridicule have come out of Venezuela. In reality, what we are seeing is simply more of the same from the globalists who are pushing their Technocratic globalization onto the entire world. Now, with Cuba also in the game, there could be a serious change-up.

Of course, one thing is very certain where globalists are concerned. Peace throughout the world cannot happen *until* they put all the pieces into place. Right now, peace would actually work *against* their goals of global dominance. Globalists and their agents always have to keep priming the pump of war for a number of reasons:

- War profits
- Keeping society on edge
- Keeping leaders off-balance

---

[25] [25] http://www.reuters.com/article/2015/03/09/us-usa-venezuela-idUSKBN0M51NS20150309 (03/13/205)

- Removal of freedoms

Now with President Obama declaring Venezuela a national security threat, the ante has been upped, and war could be the result. This is what we are supposed to think and worry about. *"Declaring any country a threat to national security is the first step in starting a U.S. sanctions program. The same process has been followed with countries such as Iran and Syria, U.S. officials said."*[26]

It would appear then that the US is on the road to sanctions with yet one more country (besides Syria, Iran, and others). Don't you find it fascinating that President Obama referenced his father who hated American "colonialism," yet Mr. Obama continues the same approach that he chided previous presidents for, including George W. Bush?

There does come a time when the United States needs to butt out of things and the fact that this option never seems to be part of the equation is a bit confusing, to say the least. That is, until you realize that even though presidents and leaders from other countries come and go, Technocrats remain. These are the folks who make the foreign policy for the US and expect whoever is president at the time to carry it through to fruition.

I really don't believe for a moment that Mr. Obama is at all emotionally invested in any of this. He simply wants to do a good job and hear the praise from those he answers to: the globalists. He'll even use irony in an effort to convince people that he really means what he says. Try this statement, for starters:

> *"We are deeply concerned by the Venezuelan govern-*
> *ment's efforts to escalate intimidation of its political op-*

---

[26] http://www.reuters.com/article/2015/03/09/us-usa-venezuela-idUSKBN0M51NS20150309 (03/13/205)

*ponents. Venezuela's problems cannot be solved by crimi-
nalizing dissent."*[27]

Wait, President Obama said *that*? According to the article from Reuters, yes, he did, though technically it was stated by White House spokesman Josh Earnest, who represents to the public the thinking of the Obama administration. "Criminalizing dissent"? That's an interesting choice of words. Apparently, while Mr. Obama is opposed to that happening in Venezuela, he's okay with it happening here. Do you see the irony or planned duplicity?

Here's another comment from Earnest that we can assume is approved by President Obama.

> *"Venezuelan officials past and present who violate the
> human rights of Venezuelan citizens and engage in acts of
> public corruption will not be welcome here, and we now
> have the tools to block their assets and their use of U.S. fi-
> nancial systems."*[28]

That comment contains even *more* irony. Under President Obama, the specter of corruption has never left the Oval Office once it entered (and he's not the first president to bring it in, or the last either), with Fast and Furious, Benghazi, the IRS, and others. Yet, in spite of Mr. Obama's protestations that these "scandals" are not scandals at all, but things created by the GOP, the truth is that there is likely something there in each situation. Denying it won't make it go away and it seems that weekly, new revelations come out about the administration's alleged involvement in at least some of these scandals.

But it is fascinating how the administration can condemn what they consider to be human rights violations in Venezuela (along with cor-

---

[27] Ibid

[28] http://www.reuters.com/article/2015/03/09/us-usa-venezuela-idUSKBNOM51NS20150309 (03/13/205)

ruption), but act as though nothing is amiss in the United States. This is all due to the political "theater" that is constantly being foisted on the American people, all courtesy of the script created by globalists.

With this latest situation, apparently, several Venezuelan individuals are being sanctioned by US officials. That means that anything they own here in America (property, homes, bank accounts, etc.) will be frozen, and if they try to enter America, they will be denied entry.

With all due respect, I'm not sure how President Obama can agree to this with a straight face, considering the number of scandals, illegalities, and the amount of corruption that is alleged to be attached to his own administration. It also seems interesting that now that President Obama has announced a desire to "normalize" relations with Cuba, he decides to put the pressure on Venezuela. It may well be that Cuba will come out in support of Venezuela and we will see more warlike posturing. I can't be sure, because we've not been shown that part of the script. It does seem clear that the globalists are in control and they don't care how hypocritical any of this makes President Obama appear in public. He apparently doesn't care either because he's going along with it.

If it wasn't serious, this whole thing would be cause for laughter. There is something humorous about a leader of one government who ignores the problems in his own administration while pointing out the same problems in another government.

One thing is absolutely sure, though. The only people who are going to win anything here are the *globalists* who create these many-layered problems that are visited on one country after another, including America.

I believe it is all done to keep society on edge and seriously distracted while they incrementally dominate America and the world. Unfortunately, it appears that America's Oval Office is the pivot point for the globalists' game-changing Technocracy.

Chapter 10

Today's Processed Foods Can Kill

Whil hile globalists have found ways to control communications, our energy usage, and pretty much our every move,
they've also found additional ways to "control" us through
the food we eat.

People are constantly accused of living in the conspiracy zone because of a belief they may hold that globalists want to kill us. The
Georgia Guidestones, which, among other things, state that the
world's population should be maintained at around 500 million people, are either a hoax or a nod to globalists and their intent to reduce
the world's population down to a manageable size.

The world's population is now over seven billion. If the Guidestones represent any truth at all, then something is going to have to be done to reduce the population, wouldn't you agree?

However, we don't have to subscribe to an unproven "conspiracy theory" to know whether powerful people have intended to kill us or not. This appears to have been happening through several venues, and whether it has been intentional or unintentional, the results are the same and nearly impossible to deny.

We also need to remember that just as globalists are busy building this hi-tech computerized "Smart Grid" for the purpose of controlling our energy usage and our communications, these same globalists are very likely interfering through a plethora of genetically modified food products. Originally, it can be argued that they did what they could to "recreate" wheat in the lab so that a crop would yield far more wheat for the products that globalist-owned food companies produce. However, once it was determined that this new "dwarf" wheat was found to create any number of illnesses and terrible side effects for people, the same globalists not only did not stop using that wheat, but continued to use it while increasing reliance on globalist-owned pharmaceutical companies. In other words, they get us coming and going.

For those not in the know, genetically modified organisms (GMOs) are often associated with studies on rats and resultant tumors and other cancerous growths. It is believed that their bodies simply cannot process and digest foods made from GMOs. These "frankenfoods" appear to have serious flaws in them.

The entire issue of GMOs used as human food is a big one. The largest GMO food-producing company in the world – Monsanto – has long been known for pushing its GMO seeds and foods. It has a great deal of money to make when their products are accepted as viable alternatives to natural (non-GMO) seeds and foods.

> *"Monsanto already dominates America's food chain with its genetically modified seeds. Now it has targeted milk production. Just as frightening as the corporation's tactics – ruthless legal battles against small farmers–is its decades-long history of toxic contamination."[29]*

While the debate continues regarding Monsanto, some in the medical field believe that besides wheat, another genetically modified food product became an accepted part of America's food system several decades ago that few even object to anymore. The fact that *wheat* has been modified is beyond dispute. The other food is high fructose corn syrup, which we'll talk about shortly.

There are too many scientific studies done on today's wheat that prove its harmful effects on people. Looking back through history, one sees that wheat has always played a role as one of the main grains consumed by people. We can go back thousands of years to one of the biggest and most well-known ancient civilizations to realize just how important wheat was to the Egyptians. It has been around for thousands of years.

In spite of this fact, there does not appear to have been the type of medical problems in ancient people that we see today in modern people. Wheat is just as plentiful and just as used in many products today as then, so what happened?

Today's wheat – along with sensitivities to gluten – has created many health-related problems for people today. This was not the case even 40 to 50 years ago, and that is easily proven.

Celiac disease stems from the inability of a person to digest the gluten protein in wheat (and other grains). "*Recent research conducted*

---

[29] http://www.vanityfair.com/news/2008/05/monsanto200805 (2/16/2015)

in the USA, Europe and other countries suggests that the incidence of coeliac [sic] *disease has at least quadrupled in the last 30 years."*[30]

If Celiac disease is on the rise, the question should be, *why* is this occurring? Why are people developing more sensitivity or even a dangerous allergy to something that has been part of the food consumption in humans for centuries and centuries?

According to numerous studies, Celiac disease – or even simply gluten sensitivities – was almost unheard of 60 years ago.

> *"Researchers at the Mayo clinic in the USA recently analysed blood samples from Air Force recruits that had been stored since the early 1950s for gluten antibodies. They assumed that about 1% of the sample would test positive mirroring the current rate of incidence of coeliac disease...they found that the number of positive results were far smaller than expected indicating that coeliac disease was rare 60 years ago."*[31]

This has caused researchers to ask a question: what exactly, if anything, has *changed* with respect to wheat itself? This led researchers to examine today's wheat and the method by which this grain is processed. What they learned was astounding.

Wheat is a very complex grain, unlike other grains. Over centuries, farmers and then scientists cross-bred wheat so that it would produce greater yields with less costs involved. However, it wasn't until the 1950s culminating into the 1960s that wheat itself went through some major changes *genetically*. Once wheat became genetically modified, there was a noticeable correlation between declining health and that newly modified wheat. Many medical professionals

---

[30] http://www.thenaturalrecoveryplan.com/articles/What-Happened-to-Wheat.html (2/16/2015)
[31] Ibid

argue that today's wheat is completely different from the wheat our ancestors ate.

Wheat – a grain staple for eons – has been tampered with, and because of that, it has been largely stripped of its nutritional properties. One article succinctly lists *"5 Ways Modern Wheat is Different Than Biblical Wheat"*:

- *Modern wheat has more gluten proteins*
- *Modern wheat is lower in mineral content*
- *Modern wheat is a mutation caused by radiation*
- *Modern wheat is grown with harmful pesticides*
- *Modern wheat can no longer survive in the wild*[32]

According to some medical professionals, these changes to wheat have played havoc with people's health, their immune systems, and the diseases that they are now more prone to cultivate in their systems. This is fact, but certainly the reader is encouraged do to the research!

But why was this done? Why did anyone feel the need to modify wheat at all? The simple answer is that it was done by food companies in order to find a way to produce food more *inexpensively* so that food would cost less at the grocery stores. At the same time, the food-producing companies would make millions in revenue because obviously, food prices would be kept lower. Thus a "cheaper" food product existed and food companies sold more of it.

As an aside, once wheat was modified, it became a staple ingredient in most food products sold today as a filler or taste enhancer, but at what cost to the consumer?

---

[32] http://www.intoxicatedonlife.com/2013/11/07/5-ways-modern-wheat-different-biblical-wheat/ (2/16/2015)

There has been a tremendous rise in diseases like Celiac disease. This and other diseases that prior to the late 1950s/early 1960s only existed in very small numbers have become much more commonplace. Yet the food companies have been very slow to react to demands of consumers to produce food that is not genetically modified, or even to try to educate consumers on the health problems associated with today's wheat.

Because of the genetic changes that have been forced into wheat, the human body now tends to see gluten proteins as dangerous and will even attack them in an effort to cleanse the body. Even more alarming is the fact that *"the immune system doesn't only attack the gluten proteins, it also **attacks the gut lining itself**, leading to degeneration of the intestinal lining, leaky gut, massive inflammation and various harmful effects."*[33] (Emphasis added)

Once the gut lining is attacked, proteins and bacteria from the digestive tract can leak/leech directly into the blood stream. More studies were done and found that the overabundance of specific gluten proteins in the old vs. new wheat is very likely the culprit in the equation.

> *"Modern wheat contains more of the problematic glutens and there are some studies showing that older wheat varieties don't cause a reaction in celiac patients."*[34]

If that's the problem, then just avoid breads, right? It's not quite that simple or easy. There are literally thousands of products on the market today that use today's wheat as taste enhancers, food modifiers, or something else. Today's wheat is likely part of what you eat.

---

[33] http://www.intoxicatedonlife.com/2013/11/07/5-ways-modern-wheat-different-biblical-wheat/ (2/16/2015)
[34] Ibid

One might think that buying grilled chicken from Kentucky Fried Chicken (KFC) is a healthy choice. After all, both the original and crispy versions are breaded, and obviously a breaded mix that covers the chicken would likely use some form of wheat, but a grilled version would not, right? Think again; if you go to the URL[35] that highlights the ingredients in all KFC products, you will notice that wheat is in nearly *all* listings.

Challenge yourself to go into a grocery store and spend some time perusing product labels. Wheat is one of the most common ingredients in most foods today (aside from high fructose corn syrup).

Capitalism is truly a great system. However, when owners of food companies always and only think about the bottom line over and above the health of the consumer, then something is not right. Care is even needed when shopping at so-called natural food stores. If you buy chicken and steak, it's helpful to ask whether or not the cows and chickens ate grains that were modified. If they're eating wheat, then the answer is *yes*. Those grains get into their digestive systems at the cellular level and are passed on to consumers who eat them.

This author is not prepared to say that food companies deliberately set about to kill as many people as possible through the use of genetically modified foods. However, poor health and even death have been costly side effects of consumers eating these types of foods. With all the studies done that prove that some of these foods and products share at least some of the blame for this, one can only wonder why it has taken so long for natural and/or organic foods to come to the fore. The answer is obvious and it all has to do with $$$.

This reflects – as we move toward the Tribulation – that we simply have less control over what we eat and our health will continue to decline.

---

[35] http://www.kfc.com/nutrition/pdf/kfc_ingredients.pdf (2/16/2015)

But of course, food companies *and* Big Pharma are fighting back against the research through *psychology*. One of the latest tactics used by Big Pharma, which seems to have the psychiatric industry in its back pocket because they essentially need one another, is to create another "disorder" related to eating foods.

> *"In an attempt to curb the mass rush for food change and reform, psychiatry has green lighted a public relations push to spread awareness about their new buzzword 'orthorexia nervosa,' defined as 'a pathological obsession for biologically pure and healthy nutrition.' In other words, experts are saying that our demand for nutrient-dense, healthful food is a mental disorder that must be treated."*[36]

Basically, psychiatrists are working with the pharmaceutical companies to create a new syndrome that actually labels the efforts of people who want healthy, nutritional foods as a mental illness! One wonders how low these companies and groups are willing to stoop to keep from losing profits?

> *"In short, if you turn your back on low quality, corporate food containing known cancer causing toxic additives and a rich history of dishonesty rooted in a continuous 'profits over people' modus operandi, then you may suffer from a mental illness. The cherry on top is that if you have the pseudo-science labeled disorder of orthorexia nervosa, you will be prescribed known toxic, pharmaceutical drugs from some of the same conglomerate corporations that you are trying to avoid by eating healthy in the first place."*[37]

---

[36] http://www.realfarmacy.com/officials-declare-eating-healthy-mental-disorder/ (3/18/2015)
[37] Ibid

At this point, nothing should shock us regarding what globalists are prepared to do in order to guard their kingdoms. Obviously, if more and more people start balking at the low-quality, toxic-laden foods that are routinely offered to us, pharmaceuticals will lose business because if people opt for healthier foods, they will likely experience fewer illnesses. Fewer illnesses translates to fewer doctor visits and fewer prescription medications. All of this translates to two things that globalist don't want to see happen:

1. Tremendous loss of revenue, and
2. Inability to continue controlling the populace

At all costs, globalists must do everything they can to ensure that people do not wise up to the dangers found in many processed foods, whether it's allergens, preservatives, heavy metals, or something else. Science is showing that too many of these foods are no good for our health, yet low-quality foods are what the food industry continues to dish out to us.

We have the choice to say no to what is being served. We can even grow our own vegetables, although the federal government is starting to crack down on these types of gardens, just like they're doing when it comes to collecting rainwater.

The average citizen today carries a very heavy burden of regulations on his back. Those regulations, which we are told are for our own good because they help save the environment, ultimately put us in a strangle hold. Only globalists and the regulators who work for and answer to *them* benefit. The rest of us? Not so much.

Chapter 11

Can Big Pharma Help?

P reviously, we discussed how many products contain GMO wheat. Wheat is not only an inferior product, but one that is connected with tremendous health problems in the United States.

Dr. William Davis, in his book, *Wheat Belly* (#1 New York Times Bestseller with more than one million copies sold), points out what he believes are the deadly ramifications of a diet filled with today's wheat. His book is filled with facts, figures, and case studies of patients he has conferred with, and the results appear to be astounding.

More and more medical professionals are coming out with dire warnings about *gluten*, one of the main proteins in today's wheat. Note what another physician, Dr. David Jockers, warns:

> *"Studies have found associations between gluten sensitivity and disorders in every part of the neurological system including the brain, spinal cord and peripheral nerves. Gluten is a significant trigger in psychiatric disorders, movement disorders, sensory ganglionapathy, ataxia, neuromyelitis, multiple sclerosis, cerebellar disease, cognitive impairment, dementia, restless leg syndrome, migraines, apraxia, neuropathy, myoclonus, hearing loss and virtually every other neurological disorder."*[38]

Dr. Jockers is not exaggerating when he connects gluten problems with all of those disorders, including psychiatric.

A few years ago, Natural News published an article about Louis Pasteur and Antoine Bechamp called "Know the True Causes of Disease." It's a very interesting article, because in it, we learn that Pasteur may have actually plagiarized and distorted the theories and teaching of Bechamp, though Pasteur is the one known as the "father of modern germ theory."

> *"Few people are aware of the controversy which surrounded Pasteur in his early days or of the work of a more esteemed contemporary whose works Pasteur plagiarized and distorted. That contemporary was fellow French Academy of Sciences member Antoine Bechamp, one of France's most prominent and active researchers*

---

[38] http://www.naturalnews.com/049023_gluten_sensitivity_wheat_inflammatory_disorders.html (3/18/2015)

and biologists whose theories and research results stood in stark opposition to Pasteur`s germ theory."[39]

Interestingly enough, the two researchers were going in two completely different directions, in which Pasteur proclaimed that germs were the cause of illnesses, whereas Bechamp argued that bacteria and viruses are the *results* or *aftereffects* of disease.

Bechamp's theories essentially led him to conclude that if a person eats healthy foods that actually *feed* him at the cellular level, the chances of illnesses greatly reduce. Pasteur's argument, on the other hand, stated that germs were the *cause* of diseases.

> "*Antoine Bechamp was able to scientifically prove that germs are the chemical by-products and constituents of pleomorphic microorganisms enacting upon the unbalanced, malfunctioning cell metabolism and dead tissue that actually produces disease. Bechamp found that the diseased, acidic, low-oxygen cellular environment is created by a* **toxic/nutrient deficient diet***, toxic emotions, and a toxic lifestyle. His findings demonstrate how cancer develops through the morbid changes of germs to bacteria, bacteria to viruses, viruses to fungal forms and fungal forms to cancer cells.*"[40] (emphasis added)

Bechamp's theories essentially led him to conclude that if a person eats healthy foods that actually feed him at the cellular level, the chances of illnesses greatly reduce.

Which theory won out? The medical community at the time accepted Pasteur's theories because this was about the same time that pharmacy was entering the medical profession. Obviously, if Bechamp

---

[39] http://www.naturalnews.com/030384_Louis_Pasteur_disease.html (3/18/2015)
[40] Ibid.

was correct, most of the drugs within the burgeoning pharmacy field would not be needed, because he recognized the role of healthy food in disease prevention. However, Pasteur's theory was given the green light for the pharmacy industry and it is what we have today.

There are too many doctors who will often reach for their prescription pad as the very first response to anything that ails a person. Doctors have been known to get kickbacks from pharmaceutical companies for "pushing" certain prescription medications to patients, so treating the symptoms instead of the cause is beneficial to them.

Dr. William Davis (*Wheat Belly*) also speaks of the burgeoning problem of osteoporosis, in which hundreds of thousands of people have had knee, hip, and other joint replacement surgeries in America alone. The problem – Davis believes – is tied to the tremendously balanced pH issue in our bodies. While it was relatively easy for our bodies to remain pH balanced *before* the introduction of the genetically modified wheat created in the labs in the 1960s, since that introduction, osteoporosis and its complications have been on the rise.

Today's wheat creates tremendous amounts of acid in our systems. This increased amount of acid, or *"...acidosis[,] takes its toll on your bones."*[41] He continues by explaining exactly what happens in our bodies with this increased level of acid.

> *"The problem comes when you habitually ingest acids in the diet, then draw on calcium stores over and over and over again to neutralize these acids. Though bones have a lot of stored calcium, the supply is not inexhaustible. Bones will eventually become demineralized - i.e., depleted of calcium. That's when osteopenia (mild demineralization) and osteoporosis (severe demineralization), frailty, and fractures develop...Incidentally, taking calcium*

---

[41] William Davis, MD, Wheat Belly (2011), p. 118

> *supplements is no more effective at reversing bone loss*
> *than randomly tossing some bags of cement and bricks*
> *into your backyard is at building a new patio.*"[42]

Davis also discusses the fact that people who often experience problems with joints are simply given prescription pain-relievers or other drugs intended to mask the problem, but not heal it. "*Once again wheat enters the picture, adding its peculiar health-disrupting effects, embraced by the USDA and **providing new and bountiful revenue opportunities for Big Pharma**.*"[43] (emphasis added)

Dr. Davis also firmly believes that today's wheat has a very negative effect on the body with respect to glucose levels, artificially raising them because our bodies cannot cope with or process the genetically modified proteins in today's wheat. I take a glucose reading for myself every morning because a visit to the doctor and resultant blood test showed my glucose levels at an unhealthy 170. He immediately wanted to put me on a drug to deal with it. I refused.

I told my doctor I would do what I could to lower it. So I removed wheat from my diet, began avoiding sweets and increased my exercise. Over time, I was able to get my glucose levels down to within normal range of 85 to 105.

Regarding today's wheat and the difficulties the human body has in processing the genetically modified proteins, Dr. Davis states that there could actually be *brain* damage as a result. "*Actual brain damage is possible, as seen in cerebellar ataxia. But the cerebral cortex, the center of memory and higher thinking, the storehouse of you and your unique personality and memories, the brain's 'gray matter,' can also be*

---

[42] William Davis, MD, Wheat Belly (2011), p. 119
[43] Ibid, p. 123

pulled into the immune battle with wheat, resulting in encephalopathy, or brain disease."[44]

Davis continues by stating, "*Gluten encephalopathy shows itself as migraine headaches and stroke-like symptoms, such as loss of control over one arm or leg, difficulty speaking, or visual difficulties.*"[45]

If this is fact – and Davis is not the only healthcare practitioner or medical doctor stating these things – why won't the US Department of Agriculture (USDA) do anything about it? Why won't they take measures to *halt* the inclusion of modern-day wheat in our food supply? Obviously, Big Pharma benefits from these problems, don't they?

Whether or not globalists via corporations originally planned to find ways to kill off large segments of the population is beside the point for now. There is tremendous evidence that points to the fact that today's wheat, HFCS, and other ingredients in our food supply are creating major health problems (and even death) for consumers. Again, it is important to understand the fact that globalists need to control all aspects of global society, and this is simply one more area where they can do so.

---

[44] William Davis, MD, Wheat Belly (2011), p. 172
[45] Ibid, p. 172

Chapter 12

High Fructose Corn Syrup (HFCS)

W e've been discussing the ramifications to our health related to today's form of wheat, a genetically modified wheat form only dating back to the 1960s. According to some medical experts and health practitioners, today's wheat is playing havoc with our digestive and neurological systems. But because there are so many food products that include some form of today's wheat, it is difficult to expunge it from our diet completely. You *can* do it though!

We might want to ask *why* food companies are persisting in providing foods that are laden with wheat even after it has been shown to create major health problems. We noted that they're likely doing this for the money they gain from selling these cheaper products and don't care whether people are in poor health or die from problems associated with it. That's capitalism at its worst.

It could also be stated that it is very possible that globalists – once they realized the dangerous effects eating genetically modified wheat had on the average person – decided to deal with the problem *not* by removing the bad wheat from food (too costly). Instead, it appears they chose to deal with the *symptoms* that this genetically modified wheat causes in a large percentage of people throughout society. After all, it is patently clear that what many call Big Pharma is in business to make money and lots of it.

Normally, prescription medications are provided to treat symptoms of a disease. They rarely attack the actual problem, but normally only the symptoms that a particular disease creates. This is not to say that all medicine is bad medicine at all. That is certainly not true. The problem may be that too many doctors use prescription medications as their first go-to action. They simply treat *symptoms* instead of looking at the causes of the problem. If at least some of those symptoms are caused by specific food ingredients (and if the patient continues to ingest those ingredients that are creating the symptoms), drugs won't do any good in fully eliminating the cause of the problem, but will simply mask the symptoms.

If we place a high value on our health, we may wish to try *avoiding* modern wheat *and* another common food ingredient, high fructose corn syrup (HFCS).

Ever since the federal government began subsidizing the corn crop throughout America (including corporate farms), corn has been cheaper to grow and harvest. That's only because taxpayers pay a lot of money to farmers in the form of subsidies. Since corn is now so inexpensive for farmers to produce, it is also less expensive for food companies to buy (versus cane sugar).

Therefore, food companies buy corn and use corn syrup/HFCS as their main sweetener in most of their products. This allows them to keep costs lower (than if they were to use cane sugar) and pass that savings onto consumers. Sounds good? Sure. Who doesn't want to save money? The problem is that we save money at a tremendous cost to our own health. A documentary called "King Corn"[46] highlights the process.

Unfortunately, groups have been specifically formed by food companies to *thwart* the efforts of people in the medical and health profession who claim that HFCS and wheat (among other things) often do more harm than good. This propaganda continues unabated to convince consumers that nothing is amiss with our food supply. One of these groups – *Sweet Surprise*[47] – goes out of its way to say that HFCS is simply another version of sugar and is as "healthy" as sugar is to us. If you read through their propaganda, you are *not* learning truth.

Essentially, Sweet Surprise is like a lobbying group, in place to fight the derogatory claims of those who argue that HFCS is a man-made, genetically modified sweetener that is completely *unlike* sugar. In cases like this, researchers must learn to read between the lines. Another group is the *Corn Refiners Association*.[48] Both of these groups benefit greatly by telling you that cane sugar and HFCS are virtually identical. Unfortunately, this is simply not true.

Not everything we read from Sweet Surprise is untrue. For instance, when either cane sugar or HFCS is consumed in what are known as *pharmacological* quantities (e.g. huge amounts), both will cause major problems in people. That is a completely true statement. However, if people ingest only very small amounts of sugarcane vs. HFCS

---

[46] http://www.kingcorn.net/ (3/14/2015)
[47] http://sweetsurprise.com/ (3/16/2015)
[48] http://corn.org/ (3/16/2015)

each week or month, HFCS can *still* cause health problems, whereas sugarcane will not in healthy people.

Dr. Mark Hyman notes the following regarding HFCS:

> *"The current media debate about the benefits (or lack of harm) of high fructose corn syrup (HFCS) in our diet misses the obvious. The average American increased their consumption of HFCS (mostly from sugar sweetened drinks and processed food) from zero to over 60 pounds per person per year.*
>
> *"During that time period, obesity rates have more than tripled and diabetes incidence has increased more than seven fold. Not perhaps the only cause, but a fact that cannot be ignored."* [49]

That said, it is also important to realize that the chemical makeup of cane sugar and HFCS are really totally *different*. They are *not* virtually identical nor does our body see them as such. It can't, because the molecular structure is so completely unique to each.

Cane sugar (sucrose) is made by nature with a 50/50 Fructose/glucose split. It is also bound together tightly by a separate molecule. Not so with HFCS, says Dr. Hyman.

> *"Since there is...no chemical bond between [the molecules in HFCS], no digestion is required so they are more rapidly absorbed into your blood stream. Fructose goes right to the liver and triggers lipogenesis (the production of fats like triglycerides and cholesterol)[. T]his is why it is the major cause of liver damage in this country and causes a*

---

[49] http://drhyman.com/blog/2011/05/13/5-reasons-high-fructose-corn-syrup-will-kill-you/#close (2/18/2015)

> *condition called 'fatty liver' which affects 70 million peo-*
> *ple."*[50]

This is just one of the problems with HFCS. If this is true, it would explain why people's cholesterol is at unhealthy levels throughout
America. When discovered, the first thing doctors want to do is treat
your high cholesterol with a *prescription* medication. Wouldn't it
make more sense to stop eating or drinking anything that is sweet-
ened with HFCS and cut back on sugar-related drinks and foods as
well? If the problem of high cholesterol does not go away after avoiding ingredients and reducing quantities of those foods that have the
potential to create problems, *then* maybe it's time for a prescription
medicine on a temporary basis (not forever!).

We are just scratching the surface here with HFCS. Why am I even
telling you about the foods and ingredients that might be harming
your body in a book that deals with *Technocracy to Tribulation?* Because global corporations create the foods that we eat, and if those
foods are doing more harm than good, we need to look for alternatives rather than continue to be under the thumb of corporate globalists who have no interest in our health and well-being.

Too often, today's meals are eaten out of a cardboard box or pail,
having been purchased from the closest fast-food palace. Meals like
these are eaten on the go because for too many reasons, people don't
have time to prepare a meal, much less sit down and enjoy it with
other family members or friends. But the inexpensive nature of these
meals hides something.

Dr. Hyman notes, "*HFCS is almost always a marker of poor-quality,
nutrient-poor disease-creating industrial food products or 'food-like
substances'.*" [51]

---

[50] http://drhyman.com/blog/2011/05/13/5-reasons-high-fructose-corn-syrup-will-kill-
you/#close (2/18/2015)

Don't believe me? Check this Internet page[52] out that highlights the food timeline over the years (see below for link).

---

[51] http://drhyman.com/blog/2011/05/13/5-reasons-high-fructose-corn-syrup-will-kill-you/#close (2/18/2015)
[52] http://www.foodtimeline.org/foodcandy.html (2/18/2015)

Chapter 13

Meat Causes Greenhouse Gases?

T o hear environmental, energy conscious, and so-called green groups tell it, if we cut back on the consumption of meat, then this act alone will reduce the potential for climate change and save the planet. This is all based on a UN "study" that "proved" that meat-eaters are contributing to greenhouse gas emissions. Prince Charles (an expert?) refers to the earth as a "sick planet." You have to appreciate it when globalists like the dear prince lecture the rest of us on what's wrong with this planet, based ostensibly on what we (the serfs) have done.

If truth be told (something globalists hate with a passion since it stands in the way of their false narrative), meat itself does *not* cause greenhouse emissions. In fact, cows do not cause greenhouse emissions from their "flatulence." Moreover, before the discovery of fossil fuels that are today used to fuel everything from leaf blowers, lawn mowers, and cars to trains and planes, there was no such thing as "greenhouse emissions." It was unknown because it didn't exist.

The more I study and research the food industry, the more appalled I become. Here are some interesting factoids from the US Department of Agriculture (USDA) that might be of interest to you.

- *Agriculture and agriculture-related industries contributed $775.8 billion to the US gross domestic product (GDP) in 2012, a 4.8 percent share*

- *Food accounts for 13 percent of American households' expenditures*

- *Agriculture and its related industries provide 9.2 percent of US employment*

- *Food manufacturing accounts for 14 percent of all US manufacturing employees*

- *Nutrition assistance programs make up the largest share of USDA outlays*

How is the food industry doing things **incorrectly**? Good question, and thanks for asking. We are being led to believe that "climate change" is largely being caused by a variety of things, including eating meat, with the main fault at the feet of human beings. We are using too many of earth's resources. We aren't living a "sustainable" lifestyle (big catchword for the faux climate change industry), and therefore, the earth is dying a slow death.

Eating meat from cattle that emit tremendous amounts of carbon dioxide is part of the problem. What is their solution? Why, we lowly serfs should consume less meat, of course, or none at all, preferably. If consumers *demand* less meat, fewer cattle will be needed. Fewer cattle mean less carbon dioxide spilling into the atmosphere creating "climate change."

In case you haven't figured it out, we're being lied to, folks. Of course vegans are on board with this because they think avoiding meat and dairy is the healthiest way to live. That is their choice, but it in no way will save the planet.

But what **is** the problem, then, if the problem is really not cows? As I intimated above, the problem has to do with today's modern (corporate) farming methods. To keep product coming to stores for consumers, corporate farms must "encourage" crops, cows, and chickens, etc., to grow rapidly. To accomplish this, they put all types of "nutrients" and fertilizers into the soil. Thousands and thousands of pounds of chemical fertilizers (that ultimately rob the earth of its natural nutrients and also limit the type of crop that can be grown and eliminate those that occur naturally) are dumped into the soil. Those chemicals give off carbon dioxides that are punching holes in the ozone layer.

Because of corporate greed, the only thing that matters is the bottom line. How much profit will corporate farms make this year? How fast can they put products on the table? It doesn't matter if the products are GMOs or chickens/cows fed antibiotics and pumped up with steroids. All that matters is turning the products out quickly in order to produce more and make more money.

But generations ago, when America's plains were nearly overrun with bison, cattle, and other animals and the only people groups here were American Indians, greenhouse gases were not a problem. Don't listen to those people who try to tell you that it wasn't a problem because scientists weren't there to measure it.

It has been the advance and use of **fossil fuels, fertilizers, and chemicals** that have been added to feed supplies for cattle and other animals that has caused the problem.

Yet today, we are told the greenhouse gases are destroying our planet so we now need to stop eating meat. The fault lies not with consumers at all, however. In keeping with the way globalists (Technocrats) like to do things, they are ruining America's farmland by forcing the land to do what it was not designed to do in order to make more money.

Technocrats (globalists, elite, etc.) have been destroying America from one end to the other since the late 1800s, all for the Almighty Dollar. That's all that matters to them and they will use anything at their fingertips (even pseudo-science) to make the average person believe that everything that's wrong with the earth is truly our fault.

Foods are obviously important to us and the fact that globalists seem to control not only the foods that are available to us, but how those foods are created should tell us something. Their solution to health problems that tie directly back to the foods produced is to treat the symptoms with their drugs, made possible via Big Pharma. Fortunately, with this knowledge, we have other choices.

Chapter 14

Remember the Emergent Church?

W e've discussed some of the more mundane (yet very important) aspects of life and society and how globalists are working very hard to create a system that puts and keeps them in charge of civilization. They want to control what we eat, how much energy we use, and eventually, how often we travel, along with everything else associated with global society.

Of course, it should go without saying – but it apparently needs to be said anyway – that globalists have done exactly what Italian Marxist theoretician Antonio Gramsci (1891 – 1937) stated about how to gain control of society. He pointed out that it would take a 100-year walk through the institutions. In other words, the infiltration and re-sultant changes in society would occur by gaining control over the schools, the colleges, and even the churches. He spoke of it taking 100 years because he knew and understood that things of that mag-nitude would take a few generations. To accomplish the takeover, there would have to be a great deal of patience as Marxists were hired by colleges, schools, and churches, and could then begin to make very small changes incrementally that would hardly be noticed until it was way too late.

This is what has been occurring in society since Gramsci's time, with more and more Marxists having gained control of the public schools, the colleges, and even many churches. Truth has been replaced with political correctness, which is born of emotional virtue.

We've all heard about the Emergent Church and some of the leaders within that movement. It used to be called the "Postmodern Church," and essentially, it is made up of churches that have leaders who question the Bible and encourage their congregations to do the same. Did God really mean such and such? Is the Bible something that is truly viable today? How does God want us to worship Him? Do we need to create bridges of friendship to strangers before we have the right to share the gospel with them? These questions and many oth-ers form the backdrop of the Emergent Church movement.

In many ways, because it relies so heavily on emotional virtue, theol-ogy and doctrine in the Emergent Church is determined mainly by how things *feel* to people. Is it right or wrong to say that same-sex marriage is an affront to God? If right, how does that make gay peo-ple feel? Isn't God a God of loving acceptance? Doesn't He want us to be happy and fulfilled? Isn't God the One who made the gay person gay?

It seems, like everything else, that the Emergent Church must contin-ue to morph and change in order to continue to be seen as relevant.

As one leader or movement becomes old, that leader must either re-invent himself as something new, the event he's known for must change, or other leaders must be added into the mix.

As we scan the Emergent Church horizon, it is easy to see that this has occurred within the movement itself. While many of the older (hence, original) leaders are still there, others who are younger, hipper, more in tune with their audiences come to the fore. Next year, it will be something or someone else who attracts massive crowds with the latest Christian innovation about how to get close to God, encounter God, or just plain snuggle up to Him in order to have the best life now.

In all these things, it's always about getting *from* God what each person can *gain*, and this is found usually in the next huge so-called Christian conference, presented by the latest charismatic speaker, challenging thousands of people to the newest way to encounter God.

In truth, the visible Church has been infiltrated by wolves in sheep's clothing. Many are Marxists or Socialists who believe it is more important to *do* for people (meet their physical needs), before ever attempting to address their spiritual needs. While it is true that we must do what we can to assist people when they have physical needs, our calling – the Great Commission – is to preach the gospel and make disciples of all nations. We cannot reverse those two things.

Yes, Jesus spent time meeting the physical needs of people, but He always presented the truth of the gospel. He didn't wait until He had "built bridges of friendship" to people. Peter did the same thing, as did Paul and others.

The Emergent Church tends to turn this on its head, making us believe that instead of presenting the gospel *first*, we should teach people how to *worship* to the sound of upbeat music or work on *social* issues rather than care about another person's salvation. Maybe we should just focus on things that are important to *us* and ask questions that may appear that we *doubt* the veracity of God's Word, but He will understand, right? We lose a great deal following this pattern.

We are taught by the Emergent Church to *experience* God in worship through loud, beat-driven music that seems to be more of a performance than directing in worship. The Emergent Church is attracting people *away* from true faith, not that those people are *losing* their salvation (if they have it). However, they are no longer joined to the essential and traditional doctrines that have separated the Church from the world. Now, the two have become one and few seem to have noticed. Because it *feels* so good, it is *acceptable* as good.

As someone who has been a musician and singer most of his life, I have struggled continuously with the true meaning of worship in churches today. I've played trumpet, drums, and piano for years and have been in various singing groups as well. I love music.

But that's the problem, though. Too often, church music directors *use* music to fuel our emotions, to make us "feel" something we might not feel if the music were absent. In essence, music itself becomes the motivator and barometer for our worship experience.

How many times have you watched a TV show or movie and you come to a part in the program where a leading character is dying? Another character, interacting with the dying character, starts to become emotional and cries. Ever stop to consider that the music being played during that scene was *not* part of the show when it was being *filmed*? If the music is removed from that scene, the emotional pull is also often gone with it. The music is often the thing that motivates to be happy, sad, joyous, or filled with emotional pain.

As we go through life, there is no music playing in the background that either defines or directs the way we feel. But create a movie with an ongoing soundtrack that changes from one scene to the next and all of a sudden, the emotion (whatever it is you are made to feel) becomes very pointed and real and you don't even realize you're being *manipulated* by the music.

One of the latest movements to reach across the United States and even into foreign countries is something called *Jesus Culture,* and it is built on a foundation of musical motivation. The seminars held throughout the United States and beyond are designed around the *Jesus Culture Band.* The entire movement itself is headed up by a guy named Banning Liebscher. The movement grew out of Liebscher's vision as a youth pastor in Bethel Church in Redding, CA, in 1999.

From their own website, this is what they are about:

> *"Jesus Culture is a global movement, awakening hearts to worship and demonstrate the love and power of God wherever we go. We are passionate to see campuses, cities and nations transformed and we have a mandate: to raise, equip, and mobilize those who were coming to fulfill the call of God on their lives. We do this through the ministry of conferences, events, worship, campus ministries, curriculums, resources and now a local church. Jesus Culture is continuing to grow in bringing young people into encounters with Jesus and equipping them to minister His heart to a broken world...but it wasn't always this way."*[53]

There you have it. Their purpose is to *"awaken hearts to worship and demonstrate the love and power of God."* One cannot help but wonder how (or even *if*) the actual gospel fits in with the plan.

The group planted a church called Jesus Culture Church in Sacramento, CA, not long ago, and from there they have managed to expand

---

[53] http://new.jesusculture.com/about/ (3/14/2015)

their base to Atlanta and elsewhere through their conferences, books, DVDs, and CDs. As noted, the emphasis for them appears to be on music. Unfortunately, Jesus Culture appears to be little more than another spoke of the Emergent Church. If so, then certainly it is being used by the enemy to indoctrinate more people into New Age doctrine, which has been inculcated into many of today's churches for some time.

L. Sharp (for Lighthouse Trails) wrote a review of one such conference from inside the event, as an attendee. Sharp notes the following:

> *"Their main draw is their talented young musicians who all grew up in Redding's Bethel Church spiritual environment, so for them, everything about God is always experienced through the senses. This is seen through the full-on sensory musical experiences provided during each Jesus Culture performance. Also, on occasion, the band leaders may 'prophesy,' 'declare,' etc. to this young generation and may lead the attendees into 'deeper levels of "intimacy" with God' through their musical-leading techniques."*[54]

It is interesting that those deeper levels of intimacy with God can apparently be gained apart from His Word. It's all based on emotion, feeling, and a sensory-overloaded experience.

This is the epitome of the Emergent Church today, selling a socialized, emotionalized version of the gospel, which means that loving people (feeling good about them *and* yourself) is the gospel rather than the truth of His Word. Since it is spread through our feelings to someone else's feelings, it has no staying power because it is founded on emotions rather than truth. We do not see this method used in the Scriptures at all, nor was it the method Jesus used to bring people to

---

[54] http://www.lighthousetrailsresearch.com/newsletters/2015/newsletter20150223.htm (3/14/2015)

Him. Jesus was not afraid to truthfully confront sin. But the Emergent Church doesn't like to use the "s" word.

Moreover, we can easily see that whenever Jesus (or Paul, or Peter, etc.) preached, there was *no* music to manipulate people. God's Word stood alone. Neither He nor His Word needs to be propped up artificially with music, laser lights, fog, or great vocals.

The music of the Jesus Culture movement is presented as a way of breaking down emotional barriers so that people will allow themselves to be emotionally open and susceptible to any message that comes later.

Sam Rodriguez was one of the key speakers at the event held in Sacramento, CA, not long ago. *"He is leader of the National Hispanic Leadership Conference representing more than 40,000 churches"*[55] and has also met with Barack Obama about President Obama's (illegal) amnesty plan.

Rodriguez' message was three parts (according to Sharp):

1. Failure (in Egypt)
2. Surviving (in the desert)
3. Thriving (in the promise)

When we first encounter God (or He us), we are usually in the place of failure, represented by Egypt. As we begin walking with God, we learn to survive (the desert) and that's about it. However, God wants us to *THRIVE* by getting to and living fully in the Promised Land. Sounds like a commercial for Kaiser Permanente.

Just about everything taught by the speakers in Jesus Culture is so passionately *general* in nature that it leaves everything totally up for

---

[55] http://www.lighthousetrailsresearch.com/newsletters/2015/ newsletter20150223.htm (3/14/2015)

grabs as to its meaning from one person to the next. There is nothing specific about it. There is no talk of sin and how God wants to save us from our sin. None of that. It's all about "thriving" for God, and once again, the emphasis is on PEOPLE's reaction instead of God's purposes. Throw in some more of that powerful (and loud) music with laser lights and fog, and you've got the makings of an altered-state experience that does nothing to equip Christians for trials of the Christian life.

I also note that these events take place at halls or arenas. The one near Sacramento was held at UC Davis and seated 8,000 people. The facility at Long Beach also holds 8,000 people. The promoters of the event do not take a "love" offering at the event to cover costs (trusting God to provide). Instead, each attendee must pay at least $85 in advance to attend. If we multiply that times 8,000 people, we get the tidy sum of $680,000, well over half a million dollars! It brings into question whether this ministry is about seeing people saved or making money.

If you remove the music, the lights, the fog, and the upbeat nature of Jesus Culture events, you are left with platitudes and out-of-context theology. People like Banning Liebscher and his traveling circus *say* they want communities, states, nations, and the world changed for God. But has Sacramento changed for the *better* since Jesus Culture came there through the "encounter" with God that a Jesus Culture event allegedly provides?

What exactly does Jesus Culture *do* besides put on conferences that – through the emotional pull of music – heighten the emotional senses? What do attendees do when they get back to the "real" world of work and the challenges of life? How long does the emotionalism of each event last?

Jesus Culture reminds me of the Charismatic Movement of the early 1970s. Everything was emotionally charged and dependent on the faith of the believer. You had to go to a physical place in order to "encounter" God because apparently, that's where He would show up. He also only showed up after a time of high-energy music, prayer/praise, prophetic utterances, and healing. All this was the result of "*faith*," not God Himself. They believed that through our "faith," we can get God to do just about anything. Conversely, it's our lack of "faith" (heightened emotion) that keeps Him from moving mountains. The truth is, God's purposes WILL be done with or without us and our "faith."

Today, we should be wary of a movement that is growing inordinately. We should shy away from it. We are living in the end times, the last days. Jesus warned us that false teachers would come in droves to deceive many.

God continues to save people. This is what He does because He is merciful. He is also allowing this world to become increasingly evil in order that His plan to pour out His wrath on it will save as many people as possible who will call upon His Name.

> "*And even if our gospel is veiled, it is veiled to those who are perishing, in whose case the god of this world has blinded the minds of the unbelieving so that they might not see the light of the gospel of the glory of Christ, who is the image of God*" (2 Corinthians 4:3-4).

The reality is that the Bible never speaks of huge revivals happening in the last days. It speaks of horrors that are difficult for us to imagine and persecution that is off the charts. Yet in the midst of it, people *will* be saved.

They won't be saved because of Jesus Culture's loud, sensory-driven (and manipulative) music, either. They will be saved by the solid preaching of the truth – God's Word – just as occurred with Peter on the day of Pentecost (Acts 2). There was no music, no lights, no fog machines. There was simply one man, empowered by God's Holy Spirit to speak the truth of sin and redemption (not platitudes) to people who desperately needed to hear it.

While 3,000 received the truth that day, many thousands more rejected it. It's not about the music, the hype, or the catchy phrases. It's about the truth, nothing but the truth, so help me God.

Chapter 15

Can Music Really Be "Christian"?

L ast chapter, we touched on the Emergent Church and today's so-called "Christian" music related to Jesus Culture as one of the latest phenomena that highlight the direction of the *visible* church. We noted how the agenda of Jesus Culture is apparently to put the cart before the horse by getting people to "worship" without even understanding what true salvation means as revealed in Scripture.

Much of what is considered to be today's Christian music is the type of music that tends to manipulate people into *feeling* a certain way, yet lacks truth. The emphasis is on the emotionality expressed in the music and getting people caught up into that. This is most definitely *not* the way God works at all and we can clearly see this through His Word.

But in today's world where truth is determined via emotional virtue (another name for political correctness), it is very easy to see why much of today's Christian music is intended to capture the *heart* rather than capturing the *mind*. Again, why are we even delving into some of these areas at all in this book?

It has to do with the fact that Satan's new Babylonian system that is being constructed has everything to do with ensuring that he covers *all* his bases. He doesn't want to leave any stone unturned, even where the church is concerned.

Imagine society *after* the Rapture. Will churches continue to exist? Of course they will. In fact, at least in some segments of society, things will continue as normal and I believe church will be one of those things. In fact, I would not be at all surprised if more people begin attending church after the Rapture occurs. They will want/need reassurance and church leaders will be prepared to provide them with answers, acceptance, love, and a feeling of community. Music will still pull people together and create an atmosphere of love and acceptance, even if it lacks truth.

It's really not enough for Satan to simply push people to create a massive, overwhelming computerized matrix that connects every home to a central grid. It's not enough that he has had globalists working to find out how to manipulate our food supply so that too often, the very food we eat that is supposed to sustain us winds up making us ill. It isn't good enough to have Big Pharma dealing with the very health problems that tainted food creates. While Satan needs to gain control over these areas, he needs to control *all* areas, especially the church.

Beyond this, it should be quite obvious that Satan cannot leave the Church alone. He must do everything he can to destroy the truth, replacing it with a way for people to determine their own truth. Once he accomplishes this, then anything and everything is truth!

Leaders in churches delude themselves into thinking that churches need to do things differently today in order to attract and keep young people there. They believe that modern Christian music goes a long way in doing just that, but it can never replace the expositional teaching of God's Word. That is what these churches lack!

Good arguments can be made for the fact that today's Christian music too often attempts to replicate secular rock and roll. In fact, if you remove lyrics and singing, in many ways, there's often little to no difference between the two styles of music, and they often seem to be cut from the same cloth. Numerous artists in the Christian music genre have become multi-millionaires because of how many records they've sold. They're obviously not simply selling their records to Christians, and at least some of these Christian artists have "crossed over" into the secular, producing songs with other secular artists that have made piles of money for them, while the songs themselves have nothing to do with God, Christianity, or salvation.

If we also consider the fact that at least some of the music companies today that own Christian music labels are worldly, secular corporations, it becomes even more important to question who the guiding forces are behind Christian music today. For instance, just as Zondervan publishing is now owned by HarperCollins (a division of News Corp,[56] originally owned by Rupert Murdoch,[57] owner of FOX News, etc.), secular corporations have bought and continue to buy and own recording companies that produce Christian musical artists

---

[56] http://en.wikipedia.org/wiki/Zondervan (3/15/2015)
[57] http://en.wikipedia.org/wiki/News_Corp (3/15/2015)

as well as secular artists. For these companies, it's all about the money and not about the salvation of souls.

It's important to ask whether or not any direction from the top can and does filter down to the musical artists (either solo or group) and the style of their music. If secular companies own some of the big-name recording labels related to Christian music, is it any wonder that a good deal of the music produced today that is labeled "Christian" seems to have more in common with secularism than Christianity? That's not being harsh as much as it is being realistic.

In Satan's efforts to gain as much control over the world as possible, it certainly makes sense for him to encourage secular companies to buy up some of the recording companies that at one time produced only Christian-style music. How can the devil conceivably seek to gain full control over the world's system and ignore companies that produce either music that is said to be Christian, or books related to Christianity? Wouldn't it make more sense for him to urge globalists to *buy* these companies and thus gain control over them that way, rather than simply put them out of business?

It seems that logically speaking, changing things from *within* (à la Antonio Gramsci from the previous chapter) is what Satan does best, and in doing so still winds up destroying the original product by changing it into something it wasn't meant to be. For most people, it simply becomes the latest "flavor," so they keep listening, even if the lyrics do not reflect biblical truth or the music drives the emotions of the listeners.

Musical artists David Meece and Sandi Patty[58] state essentially that the problem with Christian music (if one exists at all) has to do with the *lyrics* of the music, not the music itself. This makes it sound as though music itself is amoral.

---

[58] http://www.pilgrimpromo.com/ywsh/issue4_music.htm (3/15/2015)

That is clearly not true simply because of the various emotions music alone can *evoke* within a person. Feeling happy, sad, sultry, sexy, and even angry can be experienced by people just from hearing music alone (no lyrics). Music is *not* amoral, nor does it lack the ability to drive our emotions.

Certainly, lyrics have something to do with whether or not a particular song is seen as Christian or not. However, that does not mean that a so-called Christian group can produce music using a "death metal" style and call it Christian because the lyrics deal with Christian or religious ideas. When listening to death metal, it is often impossible to understand what lyrics are being "sung" because most of the time it sounds like the lead "singer" is growling under his breath!

The band *Avenged Sevenfold* is a secular group. However, a number of the band members (both past and present) have Roman Catholic backgrounds. Their lifestyles as musicians are far removed from anything that even smacks of Christianity, yet the lyrics of many of their songs deal with ideas and concepts found in Scripture. In fact, the very name of the band is taken from the event in which Cain tragically killed his brother Abel. Afterwards God said if anyone took Cain's life, he would be avenged sevenfold for it (cf. Genesis 4:15).

A great deal of blending has been happening between the world's music and what is considered to be Christian music. Today's music – both pagan (secular) and Christian – is replete with lyrical concepts and even theology that is contained in Scripture, but usually with a bit of a twist (as Satan is wont to do). Since Satan knows the Bible better than most, that fact should not surprise us at all.

Too many Christian songs used in church services are often very secular sounding. As a drummer (and singer), I have struggled with my own involvement in choirs and church bands. There was a time when the use of drums and other instruments *added* to the orchestration in church, much like a symphony. When hymns were played, drums were mostly used to maintain a military-style beat (think of "Onward Christian Soldiers," for example).

Eventually, music began to switch styles and choruses became part of the church service. Songs like "Majesty," "Shine, Jesus, Shine" and other songs were sung as a form of praise to God. As a drummer, I was fine with both styles, especially since most lyrics were taken directly from Scripture.

However, even before the Emergent Church movement took center stage, pushing biblical exegesis to the background and replacing it with "discussions" and "questions," music took an interesting turn. More and more music that was played and sung in church services became "meandering," for the lack of a better word, lacking firm biblical truth.

The style of singing led by worship leaders became *breathier*, for both men and women. Today, many artists sound as though they are overcome with emotion to the point of the listener not even being able to understand the words.

Church leaders wrongly believe that if we want to keep young people engaged in the church, we have to make church as palatable for them as possible. What better way to do that than make the church music sound sexy like the music that they listen to when they're not in church?

One particular writer talks about how "sexy" some Christian music is today. He notes that a woman friend of his admitted to him (quietly, under her breath) that she found *"traditional old school gospel music [aka rhythm and blues] unbearably sexy."* [59] She apparently felt guilty about it but was glad she said it. He admitted that there was often a

---

[59] http://www.wonderingsound.com/spotlight/make-my-funk-the-g-funk-is-gospel-music-sexy/ (3/15/2015)

"thin" line between the "sacred and profane." There *shouldn't* be, but there you have it.

The man to whom the woman confided added, "*For me, the conflation of gospel music with sensuality goes back to the first gospel tune I absolutely fell in love with, a song that opened my heart entirely to gospel music...'Touch the Hem of His Garment,' by Sam Cooke with the Soul Stirrers.*"[60]

The problem, of course, is that what he is talking about is a style of music that Sam Cooke was involved in called rhythm and blues (R&B), not traditional hymns, or what is known today as *Soul*. Just because an artist sings a song that has what some believe are Christian or biblical lyrics does not mean that the song itself is *Christian*, as if a song could be Christian or not.

Ultimately, it would appear that Satan has gained a foothold in the church through music. Music certainly *does* break down barriers, as numerous artists on the Christian label claim. Music can also eliminate *inhibitions* and make us feel like we have encountered God, even when we have NOT. Music makes us feel good about ourselves. It gives us an emotional charge that can lack truth and substance, just what Satan wants.

Again, we need to fully comprehend that Satan leaves no stone unturned. If we are naïve enough to believe that he stays *away* from the church and takes a "hands off" approach, then we are naïve indeed. We need to remember that Satan is building his kingdom – Babylon Redux – which will ultimately provide his spiritual son (Antichrist) with the power and throne to rule the entire earth, including those in our churches today (the "church"). Of course, this will happen only as God allows, but it *is* happening.

---

[60] [60] http://www.wonderingsound.com/spotlight/make-my-funk-the-g-funk-is-gospel-music-sexy/ (3/15/2015)

Chapter 16

Worshiping the Creature

W e have talked about many things so far, from Satan's new system of Babylon to the coming Rapture and the effect it will have on the increase of lawlessness in the world, along with how the food supply has been seriously tainted with GMOs, preservatives, and other things that are destroying our immune systems and creating terrible health deficits in millions of people. These are important issues that we need to be aware of today.

We have also discussed the ramifications of the "Smart Grid" that is under construction and will get and keep us all connected to it via Wi-Fi, whether we like it or not. This is all coupled to the false narrative of "climate change," which used to be called "Global Warming" and has absolutely no basis in fact. It will continue to be pushed because globalists are getting things done because of it. Hardcore environmentalist groups want nothing more than to teach all humanity that we need to be "worshiping" the earth, not using it. The earth should be treated as sacred. This is satanic to its core because it reverses God's created order in which man is the apex and everything else, including the earth, falls *under* man's dominance.

Romans 1:25 informs us of the transition that people go through as they reject God.

> *"For they exchanged the truth of God for a lie, and worshiped and served the creature rather than the Creator, who is blessed forever. Amen."*

People ultimately arrive to a point where they are busy worshiping the creature (or the created thing) rather than (or more than) the Creator. This is the sad tragedy that occurs in the lives of those who yearn to be "free" of even any thought of the one, true God.

Certainly, we need to be good stewards of all that God has given us in the earth, but it has been the globalists themselves (through the companies they own) who have played havoc with God's Creation. They have unmercifully destroyed aspects of the earth, but now that they have made their *billions*, they want consumers to think that "climate change" is really due to the average person using so many products and having so little concern for how this earth has been abused.

Globalists have destroyed while placing the blame directly on us. We, like the earth, have been at their disposal. We've had little to no control over what globalists have done in their efforts to become exceedingly wealthy in order to build their kingdoms here on earth.

Globalists have used everything at their fingertips to become as rich as possible and enjoy lifestyles that are way beyond the reach of most of us. Yet, they tell us that we need to use less, we need to recycle more, and we need to go without. Do you think for one moment they are as concerned about saving the planet as they want us to be? Do you believe that they are as diligent at recycling as they are trying to force us to be?

The duplicity and outright hypocrisy of these globalists is astounding. They have everything they want and yet to save what's left of this planet for *their* offspring, we "serfs" must conserve, save, or do without altogether. This is their thinking and it is why they have been implementing their plan for world domination for centuries now. It's only because of modern technology that they have been able to get as far along as they are now.

There are many other things happening in society, like the government's continual war on guns, the attempts at banning certain ammo types, the reduction of our First Amendment rights, and more. All of these things together are creating an atmosphere in the world that is leading global society to a point where a globalist takeover cannot be that far away.

Once the Rapture occurs, the restraining force of the true Church will no longer be here as a vehicle for the Holy Spirit to work in and through. Once this happens, the level of lawlessness will rise dramatically and globalists will be able to achieve then at lightning speed what they have been working on for hundreds of years.

Christians today cannot waste their time trying to change things nationally. While we can be involved to make some changes locally, in our small towns and neighborhoods, our calling is to fulfill the Great Commission, not to be involved in political change. The individuals who stood during the 1980s and made speeches telling Christians to get involved politically to "take America back" were *wrong*, in this author's opinion. Because of it, how many Christians got so involved in politics that evangelizing the unsaved went by the wayside?

As society continues to change drastically, resulting in an overall increase of lawlessness, the Rapture will make it so much easier for the enemy of our souls – Satan – to do what he needs to do in order to build that kingdom to rule through his spiritual son. It won't matter whether the time between the Rapture and the start of the Tribulation will be short or long, but for the people living on earth during that period leading up to the start of the Tribulation, things will change so fast, heads will spin.

We'll spend the remainder of this book discussing the event that starts the Tribulation as well as the individual events that occur *inside* of it. This earth and all the people living here then will go through the worst period of time in the history of this planet. It will be very bumpy ride, and sadly, most will not get through it alive.

Chapter 17

After the Rapture, the 70th Week

A s previously noted, the Rapture does *not* start the coming Tribulation. Another event does that. Beyond this, once the Rapture occurs, we still don't know how long it will be before the Tribulation actually begins. It could take a while...or not. The timing is in God's hands. It all depends upon God's timetable and He has not told us exactly *when* the Tribulation will start. He has only told us the exact event that will *start* it. We also know that once the Tribulation begins, that is the start of the final or last week remaining of the 70-week period discussed in Daniel 9. It is important to understand this.

Let's look at the text to see what we can learn from Daniel. The text I'm referring to is found in Daniel 9:24-27. Here it is from the King James Bible.

> *"24 Seventy weeks are determined upon thy people and upon thy holy city, to finish the transgression, and to make an end of sins, and to make reconciliation for iniquity, and to bring in everlasting righteousness, and to seal up the vision and prophecy, and to anoint the most Holy.*
>
> *"25 Know therefore and understand, [that] from the going forth of the commandment to restore and to build Jerusalem unto the Messiah the Prince [shall be] seven weeks, and threescore and two weeks: the street shall be built again, and the wall, even in troublous times.*
>
> *"26 And after threescore and two weeks shall Messiah be cut off, but not for himself: and the people of the prince that shall come shall destroy the city and the sanctuary; and the end thereof [shall be] with a flood, and unto the end of the war desolations are determined.*
>
> *"27 And he shall confirm the covenant with many for one week: and in the midst of the week he shall cause the sacrifice and the oblation to cease, and for the overspreading of abominations he shall make [it] desolate, even until the consummation, and that determined shall be poured upon the desolate."*

The first thing we learn is that there is a time period which the Bible refers to as 70 <u>weeks</u>. Of course, we need to ask the question: are these actual *weeks* or do they represent another aspect of time? As it turns out, the Hebrew word we read as "weeks" *should* have been translated "sevens." That would mean that 70 *sevens* were deter-

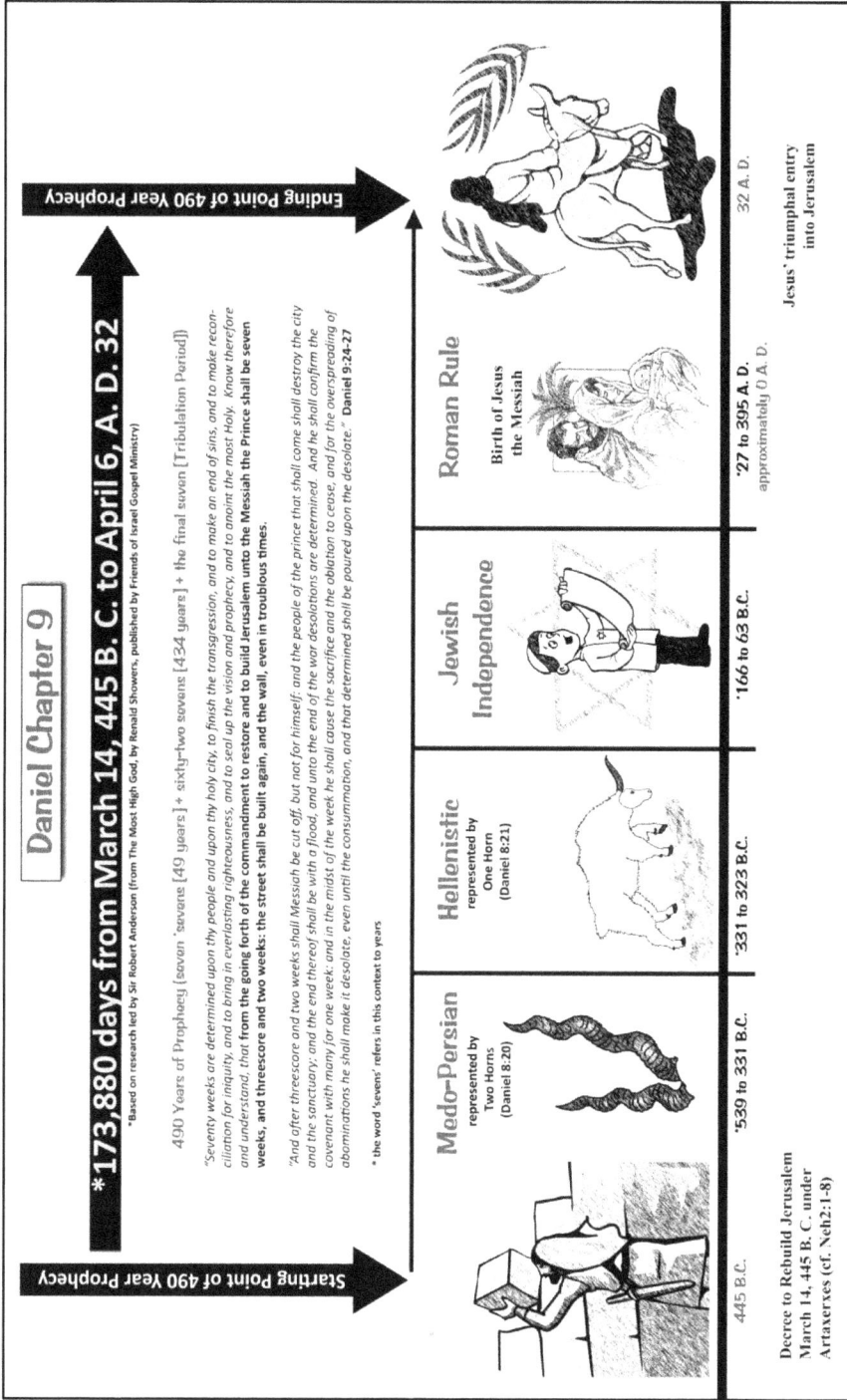

Daniel Chapter 9

*173,880 days from March 14, 445 B. C. to April 6, A. D. 32

*Based on research led by Sir Robert Anderson (from The Most High God, by Renald Showers, published by Friends of Israel Gospel Ministry)

490 Years of Prophecy [*savan* 'savane [49 years] + sixty-two sevans [434 years] + the final seven [Tribulation Period]]

"Seventy weeks are determined upon thy people and upon thy holy city, to finish the transgression, and to make an end of sins, and to make reconciliation for iniquity, and to bring in everlasting righteousness, and to seal up the vision and prophecy, and to anoint the most Holy. Know therefore and understand, that from the going forth of the commandment to restore and to build Jerusalem unto the Messiah the Prince shall be seven weeks, and threescore and two weeks: the street shall be built again, and the wall, even in troublous times.

"And after threescore and two weeks shall Messiah be cut off, but not for himself; and the people of the prince that shall come shall destroy the city and the sanctuary: and the end thereof shall be with a flood, and unto the end of the war desolations are determined. And he shall confirm the covenant with many for one week: and in the midst of the week he shall cause the sacrifice and the oblation to cease, and for the overspreading of abominations he shall make it desolate, even until the consummation, and that determined shall be poured upon the desolate." **Daniel 9:24-27**

* the word 'sevens' refers in this context to years

Starting Point of 490 Year Prophecy

Ending Point of 490 Year Prophecy

Medo-Persian	Hellenistic	Jewish Independence	Roman Rule
represented by Two Horns (Daniel 8:20)	represented by One Horn (Daniel 8:21)		Birth of Jesus the Messiah
*539 to 331 B.C.	*331 to 323 B.C.	*166 to 63 B.C.	*27 to 395 A. D. approximately O A. D.

445 B.C.

Decree to Rebuild Jerusalem March 14, 445 B. C. under Artaxerxes (cf. Neh2:1-8)

32 A. D.

Jesus' triumphal entry into Jerusalem

mined. But what does *that* mean? It means simply that 70 *groups* of sevens is what we are talking about. Still, 70 *what?*

In the *context* of the chapter, it is clear that the angel is referring to *years.* Daniel knew from the prophet Jeremiah that the 70-year captivity was almost over and soon Israel would be released from their bondage to Babylon, allowing Jews to go back to Israel and Jerusalem. But Gabriel comes along and says that even though the Israelites would be released from their physical captivity, parts of Israel – Jerusalem and the Temple Mount – would have to deal with another form of captivity.

As it turns out, Gabriel is saying that 70 *sevens* – or 70 groups of seven years, totaling 490 years – is the time that God has given in which Israel's Jerusalem will be trampled by the Gentile nations.

If that's the case, how is it possible to *still* be in these weeks? Why didn't they end a long time ago? Certainly, 490 years would have come and gone since the time of Daniel, right? It's a good question, and one that deserves an answer. The answer is simple: there was a *break* or gap between the 69th and 70th weeks. We'll get to that in a moment as well. The break between these weeks only shows us that a break does indeed exist. The Lord did not tell us when the break would *end* as far as a specific date, but He did tell us of a specific event. We know that when this specific event occurs, the Tribulation (aka the 70th "week" of Daniel 9:27) will begin. Let me emphasize that we do **not** know when that event will take place. We only know that it is the event that causes the Tribulation to start.

As far as Daniel goes, we have tremendous information, but God has not seen fit to tell us specific dates regarding the start of the Tribulation. In the meantime, we must be content with what He *has* provided to us. Let's take a look at the text up close and personal.

After verse 24, which, as I mentioned, points out the fact that a total of 70 weeks (or 70 sevens or 70 times seven) are set aside for Israel, verse 25 provides more detail. Included in these 70 weeks is the rebuilding of Jerusalem (fulfilled in Ezra and Nehemiah) until the Messiah's First Advent (Triumphal Entry, Matthew 21:1-11, Mark 11:1-11, Luke 19:28-44, and John 12:12-19).

A good amount of research has been done on this by Bible scholars (see chart on page 132. There were a number of official decrees to rebuild Jerusalem issued by several rulers. The actual decree that the angel is referring to in the text was the one issued by Artaxerxes that called for the rebuilding in **March 14, 445 BC**. From that date all the way until Jesus presented Himself as Messiah to Israel a few days before the Passover in what has become known as the **Triumphal Entry**, there were a total of **173,880 days** (March 14, 445 BC to April 6, AD 32).

This covers exactly the 69-year period of time, if we reckon by the Jewish calendar, which used **360** days as opposed to our 365 days per year. This would be 483 years times 360, equaling the 173,880 days.

Please note that in verse 25 of Daniel 9, we see the phrase *"seven weeks and sixty-two weeks."*

> *"So you are to know and discern that from the issuing of a decree to restore and rebuild Jerusalem until Messiah the Prince there will be **seven weeks and sixty-two weeks**; it will be built again, with plaza and moat, even in times of distress."* (Emphasis added)

Seven "weeks" equals 49 years (7 x 7). The second number, is 62 weeks, or 434 years. Together (there is no break between these two numbers), they equal 483 years (49 + 434). This leaves one set of seven years to go, bringing it to 490

The 70 "Weeks/Sevens" of Daniel 9

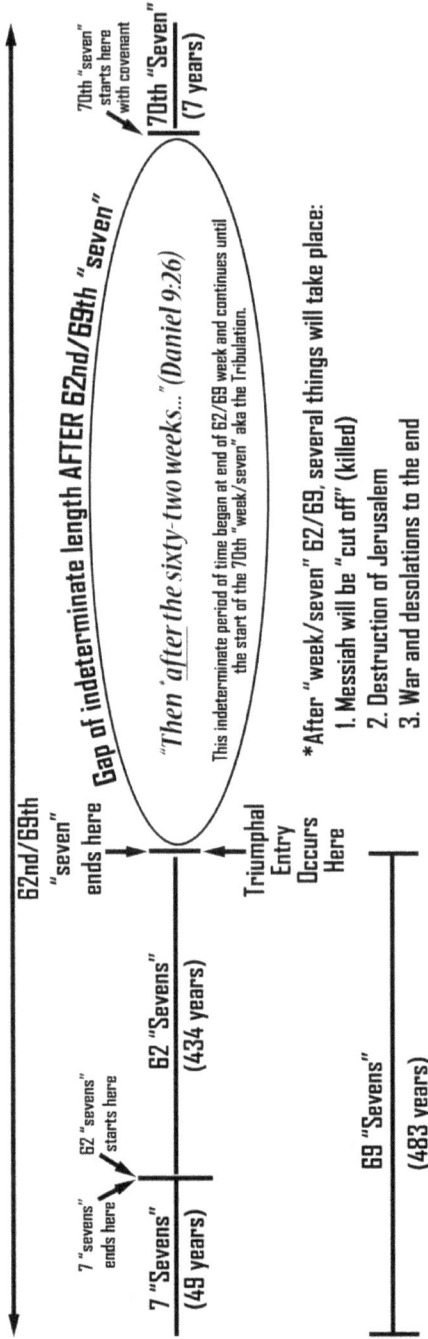

7 "sevens" ends here

62 "sevens" starts here

62nd/69th "seven" ends here

70th "seven" starts here with covenant

Gap of indeterminate length AFTER 62nd/69th "seven"

7 "Sevens" (49 years)

62 "Sevens" (434 years)

70th "Seven" (7 years)

69 "Sevens" (483 years)

Triumphal Entry Occurs Here

"Then 'after the sixty-two weeks...'"(Daniel 9:26)

This indeterminate period of time began at end of 62/69 week and continues until the start of the 70th "week/seven" aka the Tribulation.

*After "week/seven" 62/69, several things will take place:
1. Messiah will be "cut off" (killed)
2. Destruction of Jerusalem
3. War and desolations to the end

Either a "seven/week" is a seven-year period or it is not. Some scholars believe the first two sets of sevens of consist of "weeks" made up of seven-year periods. However, when they arrive to the final, 70th week, all of a sudden, that "week" becomes 2,000 years or more covering the distance between the crucifixion of Jesus and today! The meaning of a "week/seven" cannot be arbitrarily changed to fit a predetermined narrative. If the first two sets of "weeks/sevens" are made up of seven-year periods, then the final week must also be a seven-year period.

Either there is a GAP between the 62nd/69th week and the 70th or the 70th week has already taken place in history. Favoring a GAP between these two separate periods of time seems more reasonable since the phrasing in Daniel 9:26 points to events occurring immediately *after* the close of the 62nd/69th week, taking us up to "the end," which would be the very end of the Tribulation period when Jesus returns physically. The three events that occur after week 62/69 have either been completed or are still in progress.

The final, 70th week will begin when Antichrist confirms a convenant with the many (Israel). We simply do not know when that event will take place because God has not told us. Even so, war and desolations will continue right up to the time Jesus returns.

© 2015, F. DeRuvo - Study-Grow-Know Ministries

years. This last week (or final seven years) has not occurred **yet**. We are still waiting for it to happen. The 70th week represents the Tribulation period of seven years.

So how do we know that there is an actual break between the 69th and 70th weeks? Let's look at verse 26.

> "***Then after*** *the sixty-two weeks the Messiah will be cut off and have nothing, and the people of the prince who is to come will destroy the city and the sanctuary. And its end will come with a flood; even to the end there will be war; desolations are determined.*"

Do you see how, while there are definitely two divisions ("*...seven weeks and sixty-two weeks...*"), there is **no** break between? They run concurrently without letup. These two divisions take us all the way up to the Triumphal Entry of Jesus, as previously noted.

However, when the next section of weeks is introduced (the 70th week), note the words *Then after*, which define a break or gap. After what? *After* the Triumphal Entry a number of things happen, but ***before*** the 70th week can begin. Again, let's consider the text: "***Then after*** *the sixty-two weeks the Messiah will be cut off and have nothing...*"

So after Messiah presents Himself to the people (the Triumphal Entry), a few things occur that are ***after*** the 69th week has been completed, but ***prior*** to the start of the 70th or final week of human-led history. They are:

1. **Messiah is "cut off."** This is a figure of speech for being killed. Jesus was crucified just a few days after the Triumphal Entry and after the 62nd/60th "week" had come to a close. Notice that the text also states that He was "cut off" not for Himself. Jesus died for others, not for Himself. He was sinless and did

not need to offer a sacrifice or be offered as a sacrifice for His own sins, which were nonexistent.

2. **Temple (sanctuary) destroyed.**
3. **Wars and desolations until the end.**

Numbers two and three are explained in the biblical text. The second item is described like this: *"and the people of the prince that shall come shall destroy the city and the sanctuary"* (KJV). The key phrase in there is "the people of the prince" to come. In other words, there would be a man who would come onto the scene from the Gentile nations, but his *predecessors* would destroy the city and the Temple.

This act occurred in AD 70 when the Romans surrounded and destroyed Jerusalem and the Temple. So when the text says "the people of the prince to come," it means the people who are of the same ethnicity as the coming man of sin. It is not referring to Jesus here.

The "prince" in this section cannot be referring to Jesus at all, because He was previously referred to as either "Messiah the Prince" or simply "Messiah." This instance is referring to someone else. Since we know the Romans destroyed Jerusalem and the Temple, then we also know that the Antichrist will come from the Gentile nations. He will not be Jewish as some believe, but he will be trusted by Jewish leaders of Israel enough to form a pact with them.

The Antichrist is not on the scene yet when the Temple is destroyed in AD 70, but the people who are of the same ethnicity and who came before him will destroy the city and the Temple in an effort to destroy all Jews. This was an attempted holocaust. As noted, while some believe that this individual – the "prince" – is actually Jesus, that cannot be the case here.

Notice verse 26 also tells us that there will be *wars and desolations until the end.* Gabriel is referring essentially to the Holy City of Jerusalem and the Middle East. There has never **not** been a war since the time of Jesus. Skirmishes, ethnic cleansing, and outright wars have been the norm for this world. *Desolations*? Consider the Temple Mount now and what is located there. There are two mosques and another being built *underneath* the Temple Mount that are to allegedly hold more than 3,000 Muslim worshipers.

Satan has temporarily gained the ground on the Temple Mount, desecrating all that God considers holy there. He will one day be evicted, but for now, he is allowed to have his mosques.

The three events of verse 26 occur ***after*** the 69th week, but ***before*** the 70th week. In essence, these events are ***between*** the 69th and 70th weeks. It will be like this until the 70th week <u>begins</u>. Do you see it? We are living in that break between the 69th and 70th weeks.

Let's look at verse 27.

> "And **he shall confirm the covenant** with many for **one week**: and in the midst of the week he shall cause the sacrifice and the oblation to cease, and for the overspreading of abominations he shall make [it] desolate, even until the consummation, and that determined shall be poured upon the desolate."

Again, many believe the "he" here refers to Jesus, but that cannot be. They can only arrive at this conclusion by ignoring rules of grammar. The first antecedent that the "he" is referring back to is the "prince" of the people who will come. That prince, we have already shown, is not Jesus, but the Antichrist.

This first pronoun – he – *must* refer back to the Antichrist. What about the covenant mentioned? Some believe that the covenant refers to the crucifixion. There was no covenant there. It was *fulfillment* of prophecy. Jesus completed His work, fully paid the price of our debt of sin! Whether or not we receive His free gift of salvation does not negate the fact that salvation is being offered for the taking. It's not a covenant. It's a "paid in full" fulfillment.

The covenant that is being referred to in verse 27 is a covenant that will allow Israel to begin worshiping in their rebuilt Temple again, on top of the Temple Mount. How do we know this refers to Israel and not the Church? It's because the entire 9th chapter (and most of the book of Daniel) deals with <u>Israel</u>, Daniel's people, and the holy city of Jerusalem. These are not metaphors or figures of speech pointing to something else. They are indeed referencing the actual city of Jerusalem and the people of Israel: the Jews.

Has anyone come along yet and made a covenant with the Jews that will allow them to have peace in the Middle East for a period of seven years? No, but many have tried and continue to try. The Oslo Agreement was to have granted peace for seven years, but it fell through before it was enacted. Could that be the covenant of the future? It certainly could be.

Between now and the fulfillment of verse 27, others will also try to bring peace to the Middle East, but no one will be successful until the Antichrist comes onto the scene. Somehow he will find a way to broker a covenant with Israel and her enemies that will make most people happy. That's what the text says. He will confirm a covenant with many for one week (or seven years). This one week is the 70th week, and confirming the covenant either refers to a new covenant that has been in the works or a covenant (like the Oslo Agreement) that was worked out but never previously put into effect.

In any case, the Antichrist will manage to do what no one before him could do. Because he is successful, he will be seen as a god, a true man of peace. Unfortunately for the Jews, "*in the midst of the week he shall cause the sacrifice and the oblation to cease.*" This is very important to understand.

Jesus said that Satan has been a liar and murderer from the beginning. The Antichrist will be the spiritual offspring of Satan and will be exactly like his father, lying to his own advantage.

The Jews who are initially taken in by his sincerity will realize they have been "had" when he causes the sacrifices to cease. How does he do that? By doing exactly what Antiochus Epiphanes IV did in 168 BC, and according to Paul in 2 Thessalonians 2, Antichrist will do this in the middle of the "week," or three and a half years into the Tribulation.

To sum up, let's look at things this way. The first two sets of "weeks" have obviously been concluded (at the Triumphal Entry of Jesus into Jerusalem). The events *following* the Triumphal Entry have also come to pass, with the third event (war and desolations) continuing until Jesus returns.

Only one seven-year period (or the 70th week) remaining, there must be a GAP of indeterminate length of time on God's prophetic timetable. We know this because of the events that happen *after* the end of the 62nd week, yet there was no GAP between the first two sets of "weeks." The second set occurred immediately following the first (7 weeks followed by 62 weeks: 49 years followed by 434 years, for a total of 69 weeks or 483 years).

If the 70th and final "week" does not begin until Daniel 9:27 is fulfilled ("*And he will make a firm covenant with the many for one week...*"), then we are not there yet since there has never been a period of seven years of peace between Israel and the 22 Arab nations surrounding her. This is still yet future.

Some scholars actually use different measurements of time for the first two sets of "weeks" (the 7 and 62) and then use a completely different measurement of time for the final "week" (70th). Unfortunately for them, there is absolutely no rational reason to do this. The measurement for a "week" must be the same throughout each section. It cannot arbitrarily change to fit a predetermined narrative.

If this is true, then the only real solution is that immediately after the end of the second set of "weeks" (the end of the 62nd week), God's prophetic timetable stopped for an indeterminate amount of time while other events occur. This would appear to be the case since the Daniel 9 text states in verse 26, "*And after this...*" (emphasis added), and then Daniel notes several things that *will* occur after the end of the 62nd week.

Those several things are the Messiah's death (He will be cut off), the destruction of Jerusalem, and wars and desolations to the end. We know that Messiah was crucified. We also know that some 40 years later, Jerusalem was destroyed. This alone would tell us that something is odd about the timetable *if* the weeks were still being counted because 40 years is far greater than the 7 years that is the length of the Tribulation period.

This period also represents the *final* or 70th week of Daniel 9:27. We know that this is the 70th week (and also the Tribulation period) because in 2 Thessalonians 2:4, Paul speaks of the fact that the "man of lawlessness" (Antichrist) defiles the Temple when Paul reminds the Thessalonian believers about this terrible man "*who opposes and exalts himself above every so-called god or object of worship, so that he takes his seat in the temple of God, displaying himself as being God.*"

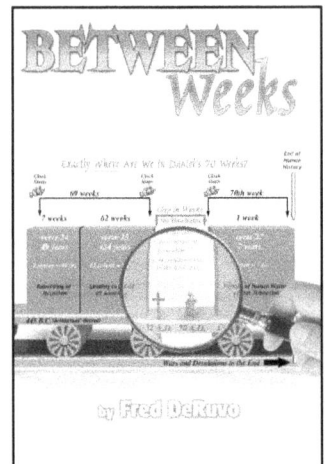

We read virtually the same thing in Daniel 9:27b, "*but in the middle of the week he will put a stop to sacrifice and grain offering; and on the wing of abominations will come one who makes desolate, even until a complete destruction, one that is decreed, is*

poured out on the one who makes desolate." This is the very same event that Paul describes to the Thessalonians.

For a more detailed look at the 70 "sevens" and where we are on that timeline, please see the author's book, *Between Weeks*, available at Amazon.com.

Chapter 18

It Starts and Ends

Just as the Tribulation has a specific starting point – the signing of the covenant brokered by the Antichrist – it has a specific ending – the Second Advent of our Lord and Savior. In between there are a good many events that are literally poured out onto this world and its residents.

What is interesting is that once the covenant is signed, the book that the Lamb is found worthy to open (Revelation 5) is opened. There is a direct correlation.

In Daniel, we see that the prophecies presented to the prophet by an- gelic messengers are for Israel, Daniel's people. They are also meant for the holy city, Jerusalem. It is unfortunate that some have changed the obvious meaning and intent of God's Word to fit their own narrative. They've done this through allegory, taking the perspective that even though Israel was in view in Daniel, somehow, after the religious leaders rejected Jesus, God decided once for all and forever to cast off Israel. It was at that point He decided on a new entity, the Church, we are told. The Church then would become the recipient of all the remaining blessings, while Israel – according to them – continues to suffer under God's curses.

The actual essential meaning of Scripture has been abrogated. We are told that it now means something else than what it clearly and plainly meant to Daniel, Ezekiel, and many other prophets.

The really unfortunate part is that there are plenty of prophecies that depict Israel's rejection of Jesus, so it was not as if this rejection surprised God. God covered this in the 425 prophecies from the Hebrew Bible (the Old Testament) long before any of them occurred.

Here's one that most are familiar with: "*For to us a child is born, to us a son is given, and the government will be on his shoulders. And he will be called Wonderful Counselor, Mighty God, Everlasting Father, Prince of Peace. Of the increase of his government and peace there will be no end. He will reign on David's throne and over his kingdom, establishing and upholding it with justice and righteousness from that time on and forever*" (Isaiah 9:6-7, written about 700 BC; see also Isaiah 11:1-5).

Note that in the above passage, there does not appear to be a break between Jesus' first and second advents. It's as if He arrives, then becomes King. It didn't happen like that, but there are other sections of Scripture that fill in the puzzle.

Isaiah 53:3 states, "*He was despised and rejected by men, a man of sorrows, and familiar with suffering. Like one from whom men hide their faces he was despised, and we esteemed him not.*"

We've also already discussed Daniel 9:24-27 in which we learn that the Messiah was to be "cut off but not for Himself." This is a clear reference to the Messiah being rejected unto death and dying that others might have salvation.

Jesus was rejected by His own brothers. He was rejected by the religious leaders, and He was rejected by His own disciples. As He hung on the cross to die, God the Father turned His back on Him because He represented sin, though He Himself was completely sinless.

Zechariah 11:12 speaks of the fact that He would be betrayed for 30 pieces of silver. The Bible is far from silent on this rejection resulting in the death of Jesus. It has quite a bit to say, so the idea that this rejection somehow took God by surprise, causing Him to create another entity called the Church through which He would continue His promises originally made to Israel, is simply incorrect.

God knew of the fall long before it occurred, both Satan's fall and humanity's. He did not see that happen and then ask, "*Oh my, what should I do now?*" He foreknew it, and when I say He foreknew it, I mean He designed it!

The entire drama of redemption is one that was preplanned by God. Humans and angels certainly play their part, but we often forget there is a tremendously important reason for why God does what He does. Yes, He loves us. Just as importantly, though, is that He chooses to glorify Himself in all that He does. I would venture to say that this is even a greater reason why God does anything at all.

So, just so that there is no confusion, I approach Scripture doing my best to comprehend what God is saying, understanding the text in its most basic, ordinary sense unless the text demands something else. Having said all that, let's learn about the Tribulation, shall we?

Chapter 19

Antichrist: The 1st Seal

E arlier, we introduced the subject and discussed differences between the word "tribulation" as used in a *general* sense and "Tribulation" as used to refer to the final seven years of human history on this planet prior to the return of Jesus. We also referenced the 9th chapter of Daniel, in verse 27, which informs us that the Antichrist is somehow going to confirm some type of covenant between Israel and the surrounding Arab nations at some point in the future.

In essence then, this covenant will be the catalyst that kicks off the Tribulation period. We will spend the remainder of this book discussing the flow of the Tribulation from a biblical perspective.

If Daniel tells us that this final "week" (which turns out to be a period of seven years, as discussed earlier) starts with one particular incident, we had best pay attention to that. Instead, we've got people who "feel" that the Tribulation has already begun because they see what's happening in the world and they interpret those things to be events that happen inside the Tribulation period. They therefore conclude that the world is inside the Tribulation period.

Daniel 9:27 tells us that the Antichrist will confirm an agreement for peace with Israel and surrounding Arab nations for seven years. It can't be any clearer than it is in Scripture. When this man walks onto the world's stage and brings peace to an area of the world that has not been at peace for centuries, the world <u>will</u> take notice. He will have accomplished what no other man has been able to complete.

That *is* the starting point and it has not yet occurred. Paul makes it very clear that one particular man – the man of lawlessness (2 Thessalonians 2), essentially Satan's spiritual son – will rise to the occasion.

The first part of Daniel 9:27 corresponds with the 1st Seal in Revelation 6:1-2. This coming Antichrist will conquer *politically* over nations. He will have a bow, but the text mentions nothing about having any arrows. His first order of business is to confirm a covenant with Israel and the surrounding Arab nations. This is the event that starts the Tribulation.

After the Lamb of God opens the 1st Seal, we see a Rider on a White Horse. Since his first order of business is to confirm the covenant between Israel and Arab nations, later (Daniel 9:27; see also 2 Thessalonians 2) this same man stops the offerings and sacrifices and sits in God's house, referring to himself as God. This occurs halfway into the final "week" of seven years.

The First Seal – White Rider of Revelation 6:1-2

1. The Antichrist

White Horse & Rider
Revelation 6:2

Stephanos Crown
Revelation 6:2

Diadem Crown
Revelation 19

The **Rider** on the **White Horse**

Man wearing a crown and conquering, and to conquer

This is the crown of an over-comer, or victor. This is not the *diadem* crown, the crown of sovereignty or royalty.

CHRIST KING

Messiah wears the diadem crown, signifying royalty.

2. Names of the Antichrist
Various Scripture

Seed of Satan	Genesis 3:15
Little Horn	Daniel 7:8
King of Fierce Countenance	Daniel 8:23
Prince that Shall Come	Daniel 9:26
Desolator	Daniel 9:27
Willful King	Daniel 11:36
Man of Sin	II Thess 2:3
Son of Perdition	II Thess 2:3
Lawless One	II Thess 2:8
The Beast	Revelation 11:7

Taken together, these names portray him as the epitome of evil in the human realm.

3. Will Not Be Jewish

Will have a natural origin
• Not Jewish

HANUKAH

Daniel 11:37:
"the God of his fathers"

Allows for a wider interpretation Incorrectly translated "God" in KJV and should be translated:
"the gods of his fathers"

© Study-Grow-Know Ministries

4. Will be Gentile

Biblical Typology (only 1):
• Antiochus Epiphanes

Biblical Imagery:
• the word "sea" is a symbol of Gentile nations (Rev 17:15)

Times of the Gentiles
• Ends at 2nd Coming
• Final ruler of Times of Gentiles will be a Gentile, not a Jew

Daniel 9:26-27
"the people of the prince that shall come" refers to the Roman army that destroyed Jerusalem in A.D. 70. Romans = Gentiles

5. Supernatural Origin

Counterfeit virgin conception found in Genesis 3:15

There will be enmity between Satan's seed and the woman's.

II Thessalonians 2:9 is another verse that deals with Antichrist's supernatural origin.

"working of Satan"

"all power and signs and lying wonders"

6. Character & Rise

Will always have access to the satanic and demonic realm.

Will accept the offer the true Son rejected - worshiping Satan in exchange for the kingdoms. This begins his rise to political and religious domination of the world (Daniel 11:38-39; Revelation 13:2)

Rise to power is detailed in Daniel 8:23-25 and will give him:
• ability to solve supernatural riddles ("dark sentences")
• Satan's power
• ability to war against the holy people

The Antichrist will be understood as Antichrist when he manages to confirm a covenant that ushers in peace in the Middle East. This will be obvious to anyone who is paying attention and has this knowledge from Scripture. He will do the impossible by somehow bringing hated factions together in *peace*, though this peace will not last.

I have no difficulty believing that this specific coming seven-year period will be a time when God will pour out His wrath onto this world. As another proof of this, please note that Revelation 5 depicts a scene in heaven where a seven-sealed scroll is introduced. This scroll appears to be something special, and at first, it looks as though no one can be located who is found <u>worthy</u> to open it. This is the key to understanding just who controls the Tribulation. John the apostle, who witnesses this scene, breaks down into tears because all seems hopeless.

Doubtless, John felt that this scroll was extremely important, and if no way was found to open it, nothing could *progress*. Of course he was right, and as it turned out, the Lamb Himself was found worthy. He went to the throne and took the seven-sealed scroll. Then all in heaven praised Him!

Revelation 6 is where we begin to see the results of opening the scroll. Previously, we discussed the 1st Seal, the Rider on the White Horse, or the Antichrist.

For now, note something very important here, though. All of the action takes place or originates from the throne room of God. The Lamb is in complete control regarding which Seal gets opened and when (Revelation 6:1-2).

> *"Then I saw when the Lamb broke one of the seven seals, and I heard one of the four living creatures saying as with a voice of thunder, 'Come.' I looked, and behold, a white horse, and he who sat on it had a bow; and a crown was given to him, and he went out conquering and to conquer."*

It is the *Lamb* who breaks the Seal, sending forth the Antichrist. He does this in His own time, according to His own purposes. Each judgment occurs at the behest and control of the Lamb. He controls the opening of each Seal, Trumpet, and Bowl.

All eyes look to Him. Once He breaks the 1st Seal, we see a scene which represents God's wrath being poured out onto the earth. As we go through all Seven Seals, Seven Trumpets, and finally Seven Bowls that are part of the seven-sealed scroll of Revelation 5, we understand that God uses these judgments (for that is what they are) to literally judge the nations for their rejection of Him (and Israel) and for their ill-treatment of Israel. He also uses these judgments to purify God's final remnant, a remnant that He will pull out of the nation of

Israel and which will enter into the fullness of the Millennial Kingdom. He uses these judgments to call the world to Himself for salvation during one last period of time, their last opportunity.

I've included this information as its own short chapter because it is important that we understand who controls all aspects of the Tribulation, including the 21 total judgments that are poured out onto humanity. From start to finish, it is the Lamb who exercises control over all the various parts that fit together as the Tribulation.

Let's bear this in mind as we traverse the Tribulation landscape as shown to us in the book of Revelation and elsewhere.

Chapter 20

2nd Seal: War

W e have reinforced the idea that the coming Tribulation will <u>begin</u> with one specific event that is outlined for us in Daniel 9:27. When Antichrist steps up onto the world's stage and essentially does what no one else has ever successfully done – brokering peace with Israel and the surrounding Arab nations – it will be time for worldwide celebrations as far as godless humanity is concerned. Please stop to consider the ramifications of just this one event.

We discussed the 1st Seal of the Tribulation period, which is the Rider on the White Horse, or the Antichrist. He comes as though he is pursuing peace. He has a bow with no arrows (Revelation 6:2). This would likely signify that he is not interested in creating physical war and using that to conquer people and nations. Instead, he uses diplomacy and politics to accomplish his goals. This is reminiscent of what occurred during the so-called Cold War.

Notice the chart I've provided (next page). The confirming of the covenant between Israel and the Arab nations surrounding her is accomplished by the Antichrist (Daniel 9:27). He "conquers" Israel without using weapons of war. He conquers *politically*.

Antichrist needs Israel to be at peace with her neighbors. He needs Israel to come to believe that he is behind them and supports them. Ultimately, without question, the Antichrist needs the Jewish Temple to be rebuilt so he can defile it at the midway point of the Tribulation period (three and a half years in). This causes the sacrifices to cease, as we are also told in Daniel 9:27. In order to have the Jewish Temple rebuilt, there must be peace, and Arabs must be willing to allow it in order for some semblance of peace to exist.

> *"And he will make a firm covenant with the many for one week, but in the middle of the week he will put a stop to sacrifice and grain offering; and on the wing of abominations will come one who makes desolate, even until a complete destruction, one that is decreed, is poured out on the one who makes desolate"* (Daniel 9:27).

Antichrist makes the covenant because of his ulterior motives (remember, Satan is attempting to fulfill his own "I will" promises of Isaiah 14). Halfway through the Tribulation period, he will completely defile the Jewish Temple (as Antiochus Epiphanes did in 168 BC; cf. Matthew 24), making it completely unsuitable for worship (as was the case following Antiochus' defilement). Antichrist will do what Paul tells his Thessalonian readers (2 Thessalonians 2:3-4): *"the man of lawlessness...who opposes and exalts himself above every so-called*

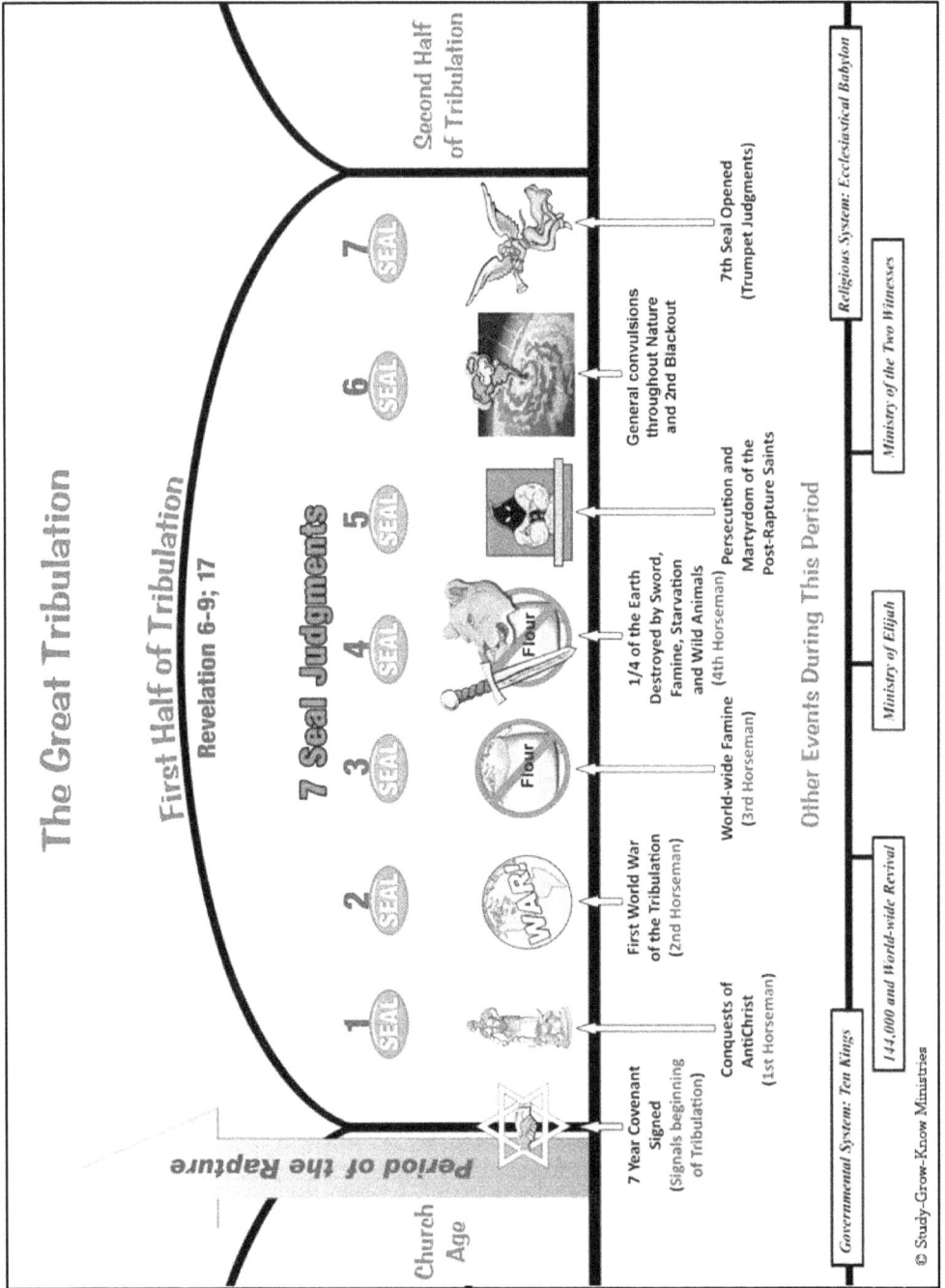

The Great Tribulation

First Half of Tribulation

Revelation 6-9; 17

7 Seal Judgments

SEAL 1 | SEAL 2 | SEAL 3 | SEAL 4 | SEAL 5 | SEAL 6 | SEAL 7

Second Half of Tribulation

Church Age

Period of the Rapture

7 Year Covenant Signed (Signals beginning of Tribulation)

Conquests of AntiChrist (1st Horseman)

First World War of the Tribulation (2nd Horseman)

World-wide Famine (3rd Horseman)

1/4 of the Earth Destroyed by Sword, Famine, Starvation and Wild Animals (4th Horseman)

Persecution and Martyrdom of the Post-Rapture Saints

General convulsions throughout Nature and 2nd Blackout

7th Seal Opened (Trumpet Judgments)

Flour | Flour

Other Events During This Period

Governmental System: Ten Kings

144,000 and World-wide Revival

Ministry of Elijah

Ministry of the Two Witnesses

Religious System: Ecclesiastical Babylon

© Study-Grow-Know Ministries

god or object of worship, so that he takes his seat in the temple of God, displaying himself as being God."

But why does Antichrist do this at all? Why not simply be happy with ruling the world? He does this for several reasons:

- God has spoken to the world *through* the nation of Israel
- God appeared to Israel as the cloud by day and fire by night
- God "sat" on the Mercy Seat of the Ark of the Covenant within the Holy of Holies
- God's presence literally dwelt among the Israelites
- Antichrist will attempt to replicate this act by seating himself in the Holy of Holies
- This will also be Satan's attempt to fulfill Isaiah 14:7, where he bragged that he "*will ascend above the tops of the clouds; [he] will make [him]self like the Most High.*"

By the time Antichrist comes onto the scene, the world – which will have been quickly moving toward a one-world government (with accompanying one-world religious system) – will be fully united. In fact, the world will have already been made one in "community" or government and will also have been divided into ten sections.

Revelation 17:12 tells us, "*The ten horns which you saw are ten kings who have not yet received a kingdom, but they receive authority as kings with the beast for one hour.*" This is *future* tense. There will be a time when ten kings rule over the entire world once it becomes a one-world global system. Their rule as ten kings will be short-lived.

From these ten rulers comes an *eleventh* (Daniel 7:8): "*...behold, another horn, a little one, came up among them, and three of the first horns were pulled out by the roots before it...*"

He is the eleventh horn because he rises to power from among the ten, though he is not one of the original ten. He kills three of the ten kings ("*pulled out by the roots*"). The remaining seven kings swear loyalty to him. He is now the *eighth* king. What choice do they have? Swear loyalty to Antichrist or die. That will ultimately be the choice for all.

In Revelation 17:11, we learn more about this "horn" or "king." "*The beast which was and is not, is himself also an eighth and is one of the seven, and he goes to destruction.*"

The 1st Seal shows us that Antichrist's mission is to conquer through *political* means. He will resort to killing anyone who opposes him. Eventually, he will attempt to rally all the earth's troops in order to keep Jesus from physically returning to this earth. It is an absolutely absurd situation that Antichrist will believe that sheer numbers (and his own supernatural ability gained from his alliance with Satan) will be enough to thwart Jesus. It is absurd indeed. Again, though, that comes at the end of the Tribulation.

The 2nd Seal represents a rider on a red horse, meaning *war*. This is the first war of the Tribulation period and follows on the heels of the Rider on the White Horse (Antichrist) who confirms a peace treaty. Interesting, isn't it?

Revelation 6:3-4:

> "*When He broke the second seal, I heard the second living creature saying, 'Come.' And another, a red horse, went out; and to him who sat on it, it was granted to take peace from the earth, and that men would slay one another; and a great sword was given to him.*"

The Lamb breaks open the Seals and allows peace to disappear from the earth. The action occurs in the throne room of God. A few short verses tell us that in spite of Antichrist's brokering of peace in the Middle East, bloodshed and wars either start anew or continue in other places. The world is not a peaceful place at this future point in time throughout the earth.

Notice the above text says that this red horse went out with its rider and the rider was given permission (by God) to *take* peace from the earth. Men would rise up and kill one another and the fact that a "great" sword was given to this rider tells us that much war and re- sultant death will occur. The red of the horse most likely symbolizes all the blood that will be shed during this time when peace is re- moved from the earth and war and conflict become the norm.

Chapter 21

3rd Seal: Famine

We've discussed the reasons why Antichrist needs Israel to believe he is on their side, at least at the beginning. This is the sole reason he is able to broker peace between Israel and the Arab nations that surround her. It is ultimately for his spiritual father Satan, who rules *through* the Antichrist.

Ultimately, he needs the Jewish Temple to be rebuilt so that he can do a replay of what Antiochus Epiphanes did in 168 BC when he defiled the Jewish Temple by sacrificing a pig on the altar then sprinkling the blood around the Holy of Holies. We noted he also placed a statue of Zeus in the Holy of Holies, and some historians also claim he placed a mask of his own face over the face of Zeus.

In Isaiah 14:13-15, Satan swore that he would accomplish several things:

- He would ascend to heaven
- He would raise his throne above the stars
- He would sit on the mount of assembly
- He would ascend above the heights of the clouds
- He would make himself like the Most High

Those promises are remarkable, if you stop to consider them. Could it be this is what Satan was attempting when he coerced everyone under Nimrod to build the Tower of Babel (cf. Genesis 11)? At that point, God stopped the process because of God's timing.

Now that Israel has been created, the Messiah has been born and successfully lived a sinless life, He has offered Himself as a propitiation for many through death, and He rose again and ascended on high, it may well be that God is allowing Satan to once again attempt to fulfill the promises he made to himself as recorded in Isaiah 14.

The original Tower of Babel was not simply some structure that might have reached the heavens. It was more than symbolic and may have been at the very heart of fulfilling the promises that Satan swore to himself he would fulfill.

Thousands of years later, the world is once again coming together as one, and another like Nimrod (though far more powerful) will lead the world. While globalists think they are building a system that will allow them to live in luxurious comfort all their days while the rest of humanity play the serfs, the truth is that Satan has deluded globalists into that way of thinking. In reality, everything they are attempting to accomplish now has to do with unknowingly fulfilling Satan's plan for

• Sequence of Pretribulational Events •
First Sign signifying the Last Days: world conflict, followed by famines and earthquakes.
(Based on the Olivet Discourse of Matthew 24, Luke 21, and Mark 13)

"nation shall rise against nation, kingdom against kingdom*...famine and earthquakes" - Matthew 24:7*

WWI	Pestilence	Chinese Famine	Russian Famine
	23 million dead		
1914-1918	1918	1920	1921

MAJOR EARTHQUAKE ACTIVITY** (1905 - 1948)

India	Chile	Italy	Italy	Indonesia	China	China
19,000 dead	20,000 dead	70,000+ dead	30,000 dead	15,000 dead	10,000 dead	200,000 dead
1905	1906	1908	1915	1917	1918	1920

China	China	China	India	Pakistan	Chile	Turkey	Russia
200,000 dead	70,000 dead	10,000+ dead	10,700 dead	30,000+ dead	28,000+ dead	30,000 dead	110,000 dead
1927	1932	1933	1934	1935	1939	1939	1948

MAJOR EARTHQUAKE ACTIVITY (Since Jesus to present)

First 1,000 years after Jesus = 5 recorded earthquakes	18th Century = 640 major earthquakes
14th Century = 157 major earthquakes	19th Century = 2119 major earthquakes
15th Century = 174 major earthquakes	20th Century = 900,000 earthquakes so far!
16th Century = 253 major earthquakes	
17th Century = 278 major earthquakes	

*A Jewish idiom meaning a world war, preceding coming of Messiah
**since just before World War I*

world domination. Is it any wonder that Antichrist can so easily kill three of the ten kings already discussed when referring to Revelation 17? Once Satan's plans are met, he really has no need at all for any of these so-called earthly kings. Killing three is as easy as killing all ten. The only reason he keeps them around is for his benefit, not theirs. They have been thoroughly duped into thinking they were put here to rule the earth. The joke is on them. They would never see this ahead of time because their narcissism is too great.

Once the Tribulation begins, we see God's judgments begin to pour out onto the earth. We have already gone over Seals 1 and 2, which are the revealing of the Antichrist as he confirms a covenant of peace for a period of seven years and war breaking out over the earth. What about Seal 3?

Things are not looking good at all. We know from history that when-ever there have been wars, they have been followed with pestilence, disease, and even famines. The chart I've included above highlights not only famines, but earthquake activity as well. This is what Jesus spoke of in His Olivet Discourse that would be precursors and lead up to the Tribulation period.

Seal 3 is famine. Once war breaks out over the earth (2nd Seal) – in spite of the peace treaty just brokered with Israel and the surround-ing Arab nations – things go south quickly. As in every major war, supplies, including food, run low. Disease breaks out. Soldiers suffer, of course. Innocent people suffer. When you stop to consider the purpose of war, most often it seems only to serve the globalists. War and rumors of war keep people on edge. It keeps society off-balance. People ultimately yearn for peace.

During WWII, there were many things that people had to learn to live without. Rubber, gas, food, and other supplies were difficult to come by because of the "war effort." My wife and I went to a flea mar-ket/antique show not long ago and saw actual posters from the time of WWII. One of the posters had a picture of a person driving to work alone in his car. The caption was something like, "If you're driving alone, you're driving with Hitler!" and the image of Hitler was in the passenger seat. The idea, of course, was that you were wasting valu-able fuel that our soldiers could use. It is amazing how the govern-ment even then tried to force Americans into doing things through guilt.

As the Tribulation looms on the future horizon, life on earth is getting more and more difficult. However, as we get closer to the Tribula-tion, it will become far worse than it is now, if you can imagine it. Think about how people – who have no concern for anyone except themselves – will act then, if they act badly now.

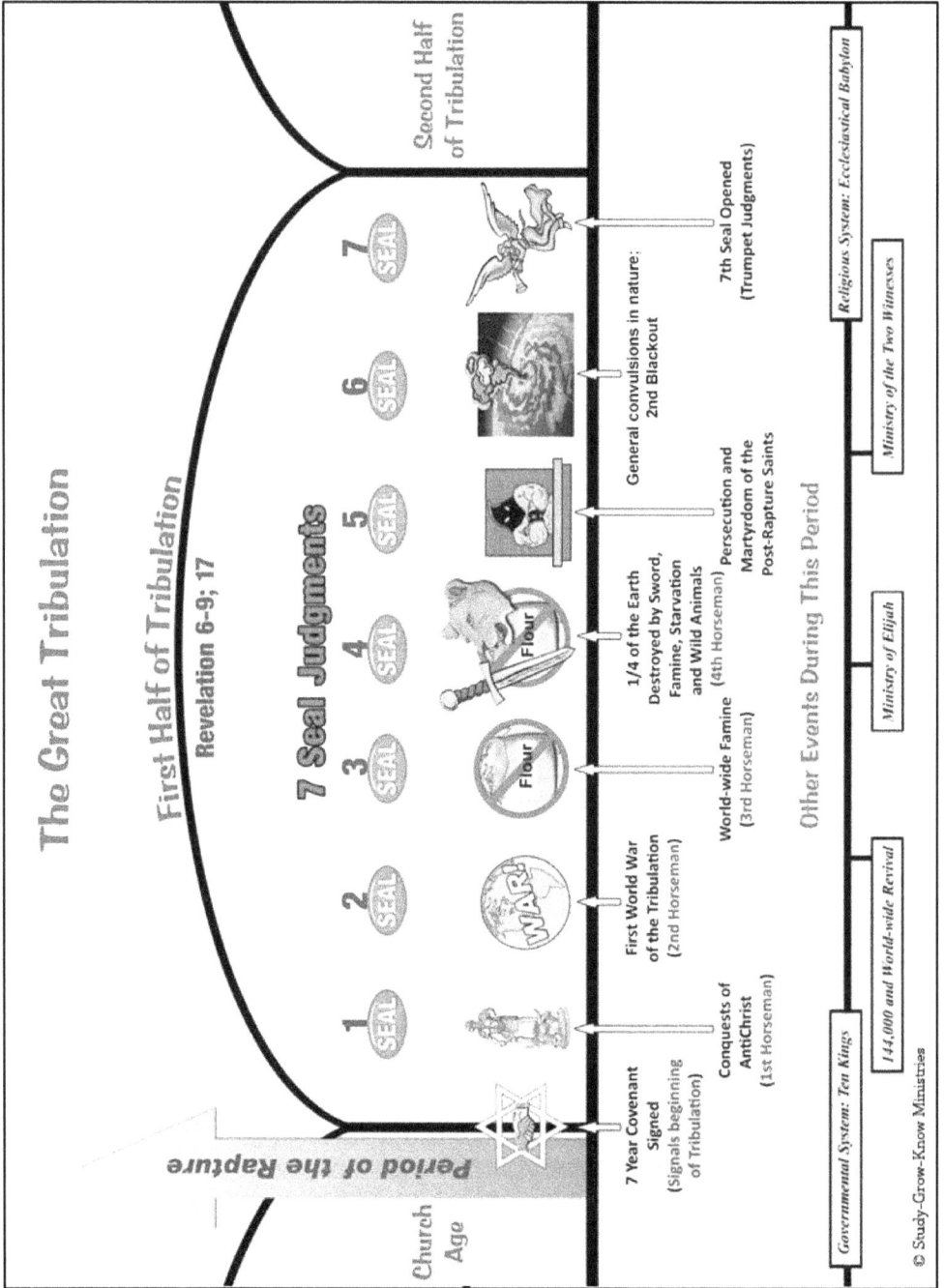

The Great Tribulation

First Half of Tribulation

Revelation 6-9; 17

Period of the Rapture

Church Age

Second Half of Tribulation

7 Seal Judgments

1 SEAL — Conquests of AntiChrist (1st Horseman)

2 SEAL — First World War of the Tribulation (2nd Horseman)

3 SEAL — World-wide Famine (3rd Horseman)

4 SEAL — 1/4 of the Earth Destroyed by Sword, Famine, Starvation and Wild Animals (4th Horseman)

5 SEAL — Persecution and Martyrdom of the Post-Rapture Saints

6 SEAL — General convulsions in nature; 2nd Blackout

7 SEAL — 7th Seal Opened (Trumpet Judgments)

7 Year Covenant Signed (Signals beginning of Tribulation)

Other Events During This Period

Governmental System: Ten Kings

144,000 and World-wide Revival

Ministry of Elijah

Ministry of the Two Witnesses

Religious System: Ecclesiastical Babylon

© Study-Grow-Know Ministries

Seal 3 is not just famine. It is *worldwide* famine, which means it will affect everyone who lives on this planet. Experts tell us that at least 500,000 acres of agricultural fields in California lie fallow in 2015 due to a terrible shortage of water. That drought and its consequences will affect grocery prices (as well as food availability) and gas prices, as well as other things. During the Tribulation, when there is a worldwide famine, we cannot imagine how difficult obtaining food and fuel will be.

Yes, it's getting a bit depressing, isn't it? But there is a bright Light at the end of the tunnel, though. Let's stay with it!

Chapter 22

4th Seal: ¼ of Population Killed

S eal 4 represents more horrific judgment from God (and we need to remember that all of these individual judgments stem from God's throne). He is in charge of what happens on earth. He unleashes each and every judgment and they individually and corporately represent His wrath on the human race. At the same time, these judgments are to be used by Him to purify and gather the final remnant of Israel. This same remnant will survive the Tribulation and will go into the Millennial Kingdom ruled by Jesus Himself

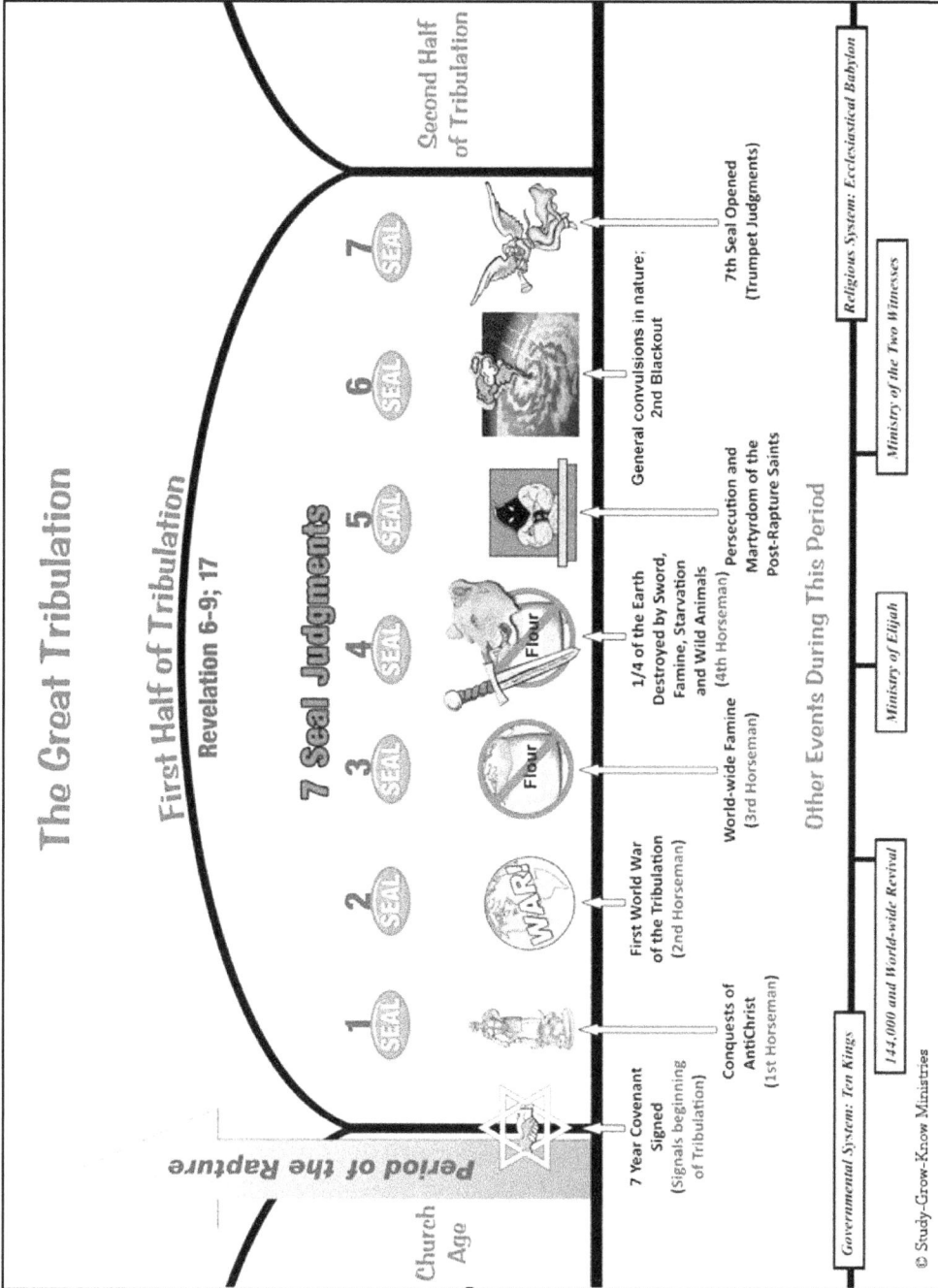

The Great Tribulation

First Half of Tribulation

Revelation 6-9; 17

Second Half of Tribulation

Church Age

Period of the Rapture

7 Seal Judgments

SEAL 1　SEAL 2　SEAL 3　SEAL 4　SEAL 5　SEAL 6　SEAL 7

7 Year Covenant Signed
(Signals beginning of Tribulation)

Conquests of AntiChrist
(1st Horseman)

First World War of the Tribulation
(2nd Horseman)

World-wide Famine
(3rd Horseman)

1/4 of the Earth Destroyed by Sword, Famine, Starvation and Wild Animals
(4th Horseman)

Persecution and Martyrdom of the Post-Rapture Saints

General convulsions in nature; 2nd Blackout

7th Seal Opened
(Trumpet Judgments)

Other Events During This Period

Governmental System: Ten Kings

144,000 and World-wide Revival

Ministry of Elijah

Religious System: Ecclesiastical Babylon

Ministry of the Two Witnesses

© Study-Grow-Know Ministries

to finally take and possess all the Land that was originally given to Abraham in Genesis 12:1-3, Genesis 15, and Genesis 17.

Please notice on the chart (next page) that Seal 4 starts getting very specific. It tells us that with the release of this particular judgment, one-quarter of the earth will be destroyed by sword (war), famine, (leading to) starvation, and (death by) wild animals.

The famine that will affect the entire world when the rider in Seal 3 is released does not simply or merely affect humanity. It will affect the animal kingdom as well and we need to remind ourselves of this fact. Animals need to eat and they will find food wherever they can. If that means killing (or eating already dead) humans, so be it. Instinct will push these animals to find a way to survive, and their first, most important instinct is to survive by eating *food* wherever it can be located.

For animals, it really doesn't matter where the food comes from, whether it's other animals or human beings. To carnivores, meat is meat and there will be plenty of human beings around for animals to forage on, both alive and dead. It would also not surprise me if people turn on one another in cannibalism in order to survive. There are many examples of cannibalism during WWII in which parts of American soldiers were eaten after being executed by Japanese in their internment camps. During times of war, there are always shortages of many necessary items, as mentioned. Whether it is fuel, ammo, weaponry, or food, one way or another, many have found ways to fill the need of the moment.

Can you see how the Tribulation period is increasingly becoming more dangerous, more terrible, and more deadly? Why is God doing this? He is doing it because of how evil humanity will have become and because of all the unjudged ills that have been perpetrated.

If God destroyed an entire globe of people except for eight individuals during the time of Noah and if He destroyed the twin cities of Sodom and Gomorrah because of the level of constant evil, then doesn't it stand to reason that He will put a halt to humanity's growth because of how evil people will have become at the time of the Tribulation period? He wants our attention because He wants to give people an opportunity to repent, to come to Him for salvation, and to be saved.

He will also use this time to pierce Israel's heart so that they will come to understand how wrong they have been about Jehovah God in their rejection of Jesus as Messiah. How can we believe that humanity will continue to go on as if God does not exist? He has patience for only so much and when the end of His patience has come, He puts things in motion that will ultimately eradicate the evil that has become a stench to His nostrils for so long. One day, it will be gone forever, permanently.

I received a short email from a person who had read my previous writings of this series. His brief comment was, "*Ask Christians all throughout North Africa, the Middle East, Asia and any other place where Islam dominates. They will not tell you that the tribulation is coming. They will tell you it is already here.*"

The problem, though, is that persecution, while being part of the coming Tribulation period (as it is in life in general), is not a sign that the Tribulation is here. Did the Tribulation happen when Christians were being terribly treated and executed by Nero? While they may have been tempted to believe it, in the end, it was simply God-allowed persecution in order that His Word might spread throughout the Roman Empire by forcing Christians to flee to other areas so that the gospel could be spread.

Persecution is *never* a barometer of whether or not we are "in" the "Tribulation." Persecution is part of the generalized tribulation that all Christians suffer through in this life. It will simply become terribly, terribly, bad and specifically directed during the time of the Tribulation period. It will be a time of God's wrath poured out on unrepentant humanity. God's wrath is far different from persecution.

We are *not* in the Tribulation now. That period of time will begin with one event: the confirming of the covenant with Israel and the surrounding Arab nations. That will be the event that releases the Antichrist to the world and makes him known. He will – because of this event – become an instant celebrity and people will begin to marvel after him. He will ultimately rise to become the single leader of the revised "Roman Empire" (final phase of the 4th beast; Daniel 2; Daniel 7; Revelation 17) that is in the making now.

When this same Antichrist defiles the Temple in the middle of the Tribulation, his true identity and purpose will be unmasked to the Jews of Israel, causing them to flee to the mountains where God will protect and take care of them for the remainder of the Tribulation period.

Chapter 23

Seals 5, 6, and 7

As previously noted, Seal 4 represents the fact that one-fourth of the world's population will be destroyed by sword (war/conflict), famine, starvation, and wild animals. If I've done the math correctly that means that roughly 1.75 billion people will die once Seal 4 is opened (based on a current total global population of 7 billion). That represents a huge number of people.

Seal 5 opens and <u>persecution</u> ramps up against those Christians living during that coming time. For many to most, this persecution will end in their deaths. Martyrdom will be the way many pass from this life to the next during this upcoming terrible seven-year period.

There's good reason for this, aside from the fact that it is declared in Scripture. Let's look at the text of Revelation 6:9-11.

> *"When the Lamb broke the fifth seal, I saw underneath the altar the souls of those who had been slain because of the word of God, and because of the testimony which they had maintained; and they cried out with a loud voice, saying, 'How long, O Lord, holy and true, will You refrain from judging and avenging our blood on those who dwell on the earth?' And there was given to each of them a white robe; and they were told that they should rest for a little while longer, until the number of their fellow servants and their brethren who were to be killed even as they had been, would be completed also."*

Take Communism, for example, which has been a tremendous persecutor of Christians throughout the world since Communism's inception. Why is that? Communism is a system built on ideals that are fully antithetical to God and His Word. In the Bible, we see that Adam – man – was the pinnacle of God's Creation. Man is the only creature in which God breathed a soul into him and he then became a living being. This was not done to any of the plants or animals, but only to man.

Communism says that man is simply another animal. Any traits seen in man – *"'tenets of rugged individualism, personal determinism, self-will, imagination, and personal creativeness...' – are not good things. In fact, they are seen as 'equally antipathetic to the good of the Greater State.'"*[61]

According to the beliefs of Communism, ingenuity, creativeness, intelligence, individuality, and other attributes bestowed upon man when God created him are things to be despised, ignored, and even

---

[61] Terry L. Cook, Psycho Political Brainwashing (2010), p. 28

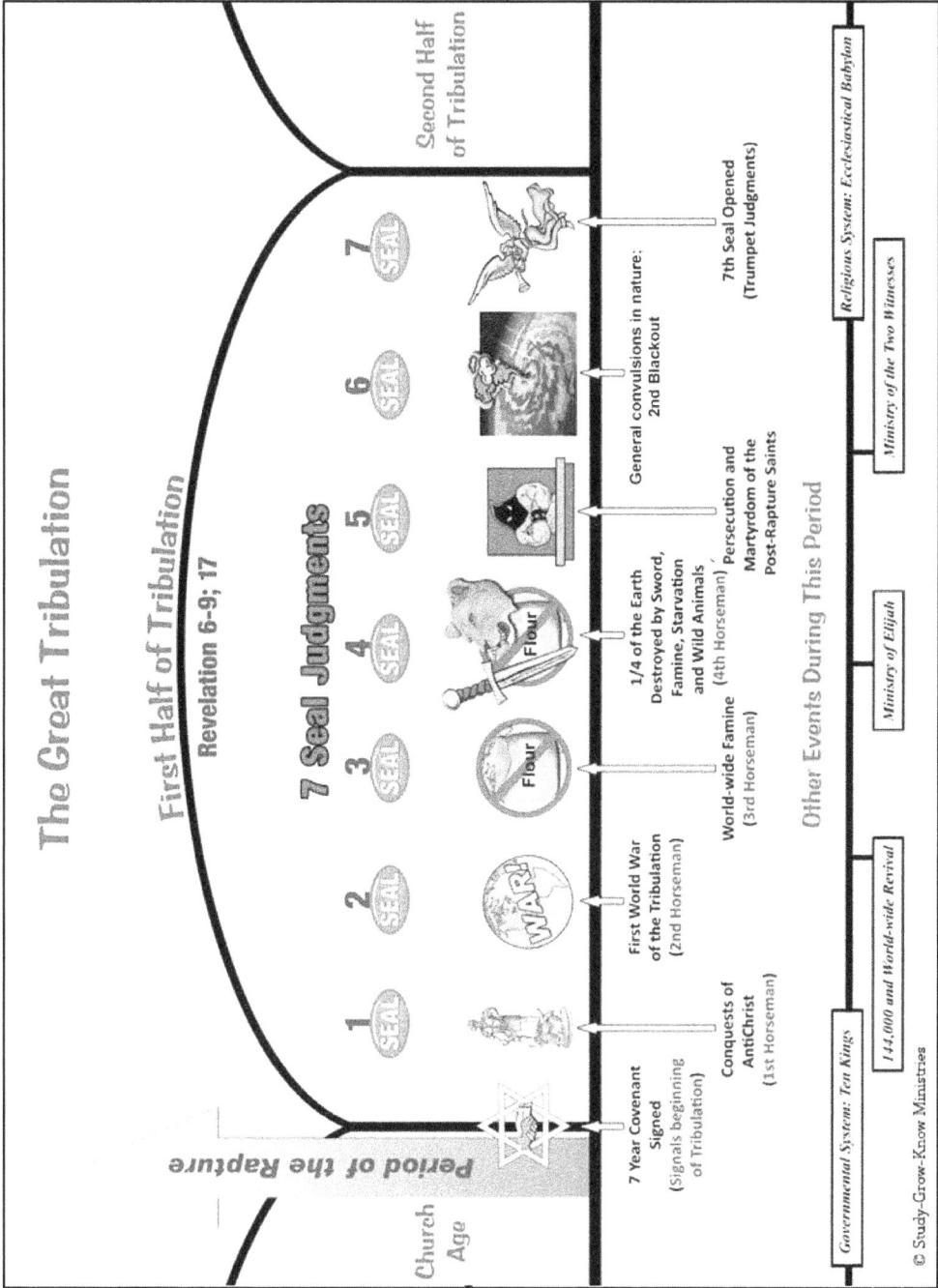

The Great Tribulation

First Half of Tribulation

Revelation 6-9; 17

Second Half of Tribulation

Period of the Rapture

Church Age

7 Seal Judgments

SEAL 1
SEAL 2
SEAL 3
SEAL 4
SEAL 5
SEAL 6
SEAL 7

7 Year Covenant Signed
(Signals beginning of Tribulation)

Conquests of AntiChrist
(1st Horseman)

First World War of the Tribulation
(2nd Horseman)

World-wide Famine
(3rd Horseman)

1/4 of the Earth Destroyed by Sword, Famine, Starvation and Wild Animals
(4th Horseman)

Persecution and Martyrdom of the Post-Rapture Saints

General convulsions in nature: 2nd Blackout

7th Seal Opened
(Trumpet Judgments)

Other Events During This Period

Governmental System: Ten Kings	Religious System: Ecclesiastical Babylon

144,000 and World-wide Revival

Ministry of Elijah

Ministry of the Two Witnesses

© Study-Grow-Know Ministries

eradicated. If need be, the person himself needs to be eliminated in order that the "state" (or "collective") might carry on as the greater entity.

Communism seeks to destroy all the things that man has been given by God, who places him well above the animal kingdom. As all falsehoods, this false ideology – Communism – is born in the depths of hell and promulgated by Satan himself. It is diametrically opposed to God. As time progresses toward the end of this current age, is it any wonder that the masses will be completely taken over by the atheistic nonsense that is called Communism? It's happening today.

Christians and those who hold to a religious ideology (with the possible exception of Islam) will be seen as anathema. They will be seen as **the** problem that keeps the state from becoming even greater. As such, the options will be limited. Change or die. Those who worship the one, true God in Jesus will in no way separate themselves from their loyalty and allegiance to Him. Thus, their end is assured if they are caught.

Seal 6 is then opened and released and this world will experience what the Bible calls "general convulsions throughout nature" along with a second complete blackout. I don't expect that many of us can picture what the world will be like with a total blackout. Consider the sun no longer shining and the moon no longer reflecting the sun's light. At the same time, the stars turn dark. This will be an unnerving time for this earth with scientists unable to provide any plausible explanation as to why it's happening.

Let's look at the biblical text regarding Seal 6, from Revelation 6:12-14.

> *"I looked when He broke the sixth seal, and there was a*
> *great earthquake; and the sun became black as sackcloth*
> *made of hair, and the whole moon became like blood; and*

> *the stars of the sky fell to the earth, as a fig tree casts its*
> *unripe figs when shaken by a great wind. The sky was*
> *split apart like a scroll when it is rolled up, and every*
> *mountain and island were moved out of their places."*

It's not just darkness. There is a tremendous earthquake, the sun becomes black, and the moon appears to turn blood-red. Stars fall to the earth in droves and the most terrifying thing of all happens when the sky itself splits apart and mountains and islands move from their original places.

My guess is that the earthquake is huge. Are tsunamis to follow this action? Did the earthquake also set off volcanoes that send tons of ash and other pollutants into the atmosphere above the earth? Are these things the causes of blocking the sun, making it appear as if the lights went out on earth? We know that when a total lunar eclipse occurs, the moon will often appear red in color. Is this what is happening here?

How do the people on earth react to all of these things? Revelation 6:15-17 tells us point-blank.

> *"Then the kings of the earth and the great men and the*
> *commanders and the rich and the strong and every slave*
> *and free man hid themselves in the caves and among the*
> *rocks of the mountains; and they said to the mountains*
> *and to the rocks, 'Fall on us and hide us from the presence*
> *of Him who sits on the throne, and from the wrath of the*
> *Lamb; for the great day of their wrath has come, and who*
> *is able to stand?'"*

Clearly, there will be at least some people who know the Source of the trouble. They will try to hide in caves to get away from God and beg the mountains to bury them so they can avoid "the wrath of the Lamb." In other words, they know that they know that they know that God Himself is the source of these problems, yet they do not re-pent. They do not seek His face. They run from Him. They try to hide, as if anyone could truly hide from God, who is omniscient. Even when they know the truth, they ignore it.

The Tribulation – all seven years of it – represents God's wrath and the people on earth will understand that, even though theologians argue about it and dismiss it today. Those living during the Tribula-tion will find life very, very difficult. They will be forced to choose human government or God's rule over their lives.

But let's remember, this is only the first part of the Tribulation. This section ends with the opening of Seal 7, and with that, we are intro-duced to the Seven Trumpet Seals. We will get into those in our next chapter.

Chapter 24

Listen to the Trumpets!

We have finished going over the Seven Seals that constitute the first part of the Tribulation/Great Tribulation. Now, we're moving onto the next phase of this coming period of seven years of hell on earth. Again, though many folks prefer to see the coming Tribulation period as something that has already happened or they prefer to allegorize the meaning of the judgments, I take things literally. By that I mean that I seek the literal meaning of the events in question.

Once again, all the direction takes place from the throne room of the Lamb in heaven. He decides when He will open each judgment and how those judgments will appear on earth. While John uses descriptive language for the Seven Seals, Trumpets, and Bowls, there is arguably one literal meaning for each judgment.

The other fact to consider is that there are many people who prefer to take the measurements and specific periods of time as metaphors for something else. However, throughout the book of Revelation, these periods of time are very specific and their specificity is a clear indication that they should not be taken allegorically. If John calls out the number 144,000, with 12,000 individuals taken from each tribe of Israel, there is really no reason to take these numbers metaphorically. They should be taken literally and the fact that some choose to take them to mean something else distorts the truth of God's Word.

The only place where we can really say that something might be referring to something else is in the description of the individual judgments. For instance, when we read that a "mountain" was thrown into the sea, is it really a mountain? It could be an asteroid, or a very large meteor, which to John appeared as a mountain. What is important here is what occurs after the mountain is thrown into the sea. What is the result of that? Of course, this is up to each person to decide. Hopefully, logic, common sense, and critical thinking will guide you.

Notice that as the 7th Seal opens, there is a period of silence in heaven. This period lasts for 30 minutes. Is this a literal 30 minutes? I would say so, as there is no reason to take it any other way. It appears as though it is the quiet before the storm, or the silence before the curtain goes up after the lights go out for a theatrical production. It is an attention-getter.

Immediately following this 30-minute interval, the 1st Trumpet is blown. This is followed by the results of that Trumpet Judgment, which happen to be hail, fire, and blood poured out onto the earth. By the way, the trumpet itself was widely used in ancient Israel. It

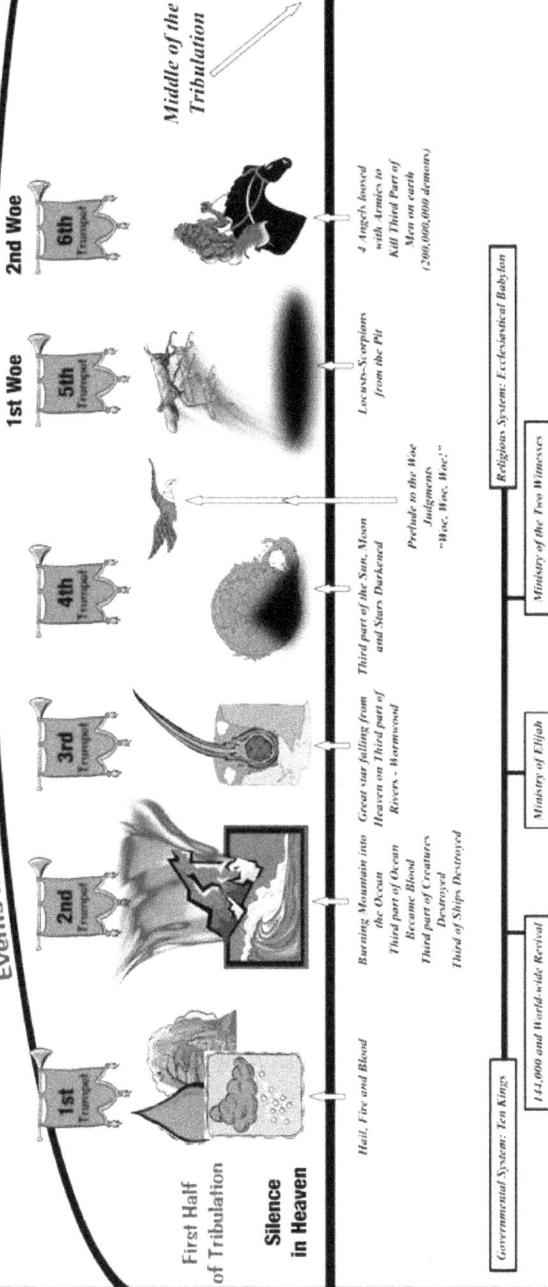

Trumpet Judgments of The Great Tribulation
Revelation 8:1 to 9:21

Events in the Middle of Tribulation, Part 1

First Half of Tribulation

Silence in Heaven

1st Trumpet — Hail, Fire and Blood

2nd Trumpet — Burning Mountain into the Ocean / Third part of Ocean Became Blood / Third part of Creatures Destroyed / Third of Ships Destroyed

3rd Trumpet — Great star falling from Heaven on Third part of Rivers - Wormwood

4th Trumpet — Third part of the Sun, Moon and Stars Darkened / Prelude to the Woe Judgments "Woe, Woe, Woe!"

1st Woe — 5th Trumpet — Locusts-Scorpions from the Pit

2nd Woe — 6th Trumpet — 4 Angels loosed with Armies to Kill Third Part of Men on earth (200,000,000 armies)

Middle of the Tribulation

Governmental System: Ten Kings

144,000 and World-wide Revival

Ministry of Elijah

Ministry of the Two Witnesses

Religious System: Ecclesiastical Babylon

© Study-Grow-Know Ministries

was used to call Israel to war as well as being used in the ceremonial process.

Some individuals believe that it is at the "last trump" that the Rapture happens, and they assume that the last trump of Revelation (the 7th Trumpet) is that "last trump." The problem with this view is that when Paul wrote 1 Thessalonians 4, the book of Revelation had not been written yet. It would have left people hanging, wondering what "trump" Paul was referring to in his letter. Throughout Israel's history, there were many "last trumps." The last trump was simply the final long trumpet in a series of trumps to signify that that series of trumpet calls was done.

While there is some connection between 1 Corinthians 15 and 1 Thessalonians 4 with respect to the "last trump," it's quite a stretch to include Revelation 11:15 in with those two passages. Those who believe that the 7th Trumpet of Revelation is the "last trump" to which Paul is referring in 1 Corinthians 15 and 1 Thessalonians 4 also believe that the Rapture of the Bride of Christ will occur then, in the middle of the Tribulation.

At the same time, Jesus told us that no one would know the day or hour (Matthew 24:36), yet if the 7th Trumpet is the "last trump," then clearly, people who are paying attention will be able to narrow things down quite a bit.

> *"The first [trumpet] sounded, and there came hail and fire, mixed with blood, and they were thrown to the earth; and a third of the earth was burned up, and a third of the trees were burned up, and all the green grass was burned up"* (Revelation 8:7).

Thomas Constable points out that blood-red rain is not unheard of in nature. *"[I]n the spring of 1901 the daily journals contained accounts of this phenomenon, which was then being witnessed in Italy and the*

South of Europe, the result, it was said, of the air being full of particles of fine red sand from the Sahara."[62]

We do not know how these judgments will look when unleashed, but we do know that these things are not impossible. God will certainly make His wrath clearly known and understood. Whether or not people respond to it is another thing altogether.

Eyewitness account of destruction of Sodom and Gomorrah

We know all too well that God has rained fire (and sometimes brimstone) down from heaven. In fact, a clay tablet that was literally unreadable for over 150 years after its discovery was decoded after scientists discovered the key to unlock that code. It points to a date *"shortly before dawn on June 29 in the year 3123 B.C."*

The tablet records the destruction of Sodom and Gomorrah, and scientists now know that these twin cities were destroyed by an asteroid. While many people refuse to believe the Bible's straightforward testimony and narrative, science has determined through the eyewitness account of an individual who saw the event and recorded it that Sodom was destroyed by a giant "mountain" that fell from the heavens, which many scientists believe may have been up to one mile wide.

Will the future Tribulation period see these "mountains" fall from heaven, creating destruction in their path? I have no doubt.

---

[62] Thomas Constable, Notes on Revelation, p 91

Chapter 25

1st and 2nd Trumpet Judgments

J ust prior to the release or blowing of the 1st Trumpet Judgment, there is silence in heaven for roughly 30 minutes. The reason is simple. Just as the lights go down and silence ensues prior to the start of a concert or theatrical production, so it is with God's unveiling of things in His plan of redemption. All in heaven wait in anticipation of His precise movement and moment. All eyes are on Him. His will is going to be accomplished and He will not be rushed. This 30 minutes really represents the quiet before the hurricane.

The first six Trumpet Judgments are recorded for us initially in Revelation 8-9. More information concerning these judgments is provided in Revelation 10:1–11:14. The 7th Trumpet Judgment is highlighted in Revelation 11:15–16:21 with more specific information being re-vealed in Revelation 12–15.

Trumpets have always been a very important, integral part of God's dealings with Israel, and so they are here as well. In the beginning verses of chapter 8, we see an angel take the incense (representing prayers of the saints) with hot coals from the fire in his censer and fling it to earth. Once he does this, the earth is pounded with *"…peals of thunder and sounds and flashes of lightning and an earthquake"* (Revelation 8:5b).

One day, my family and I were sitting on the couch watching TV. All of a sudden, there was this tremendously loud crack or boom in the night sky. It was thunder I have never heard before, and I have spent years on the east coast and am familiar with the thunder storms here. It was just a very odd-sounding peal of thunder, as though a concen-trated explosion had gone off in the sky. All of us jumped up com-pletely startled, even though it had already been raining with thun-der and lightning. This was very different.

This is what this would be like, but far worse. It is God's way of get-ting the attention of those on the earth for what's coming next. After this, the first angel sounded his Trumpet Judgment and we learn from Revelation 8:7 that *"…there came hail and fire, mixed with blood, and they were thrown to the earth; and a third of the earth was burned up, and a third of the trees were burned up, and all the green grass was burned up."*

The angel who threw the contents of his censer to earth signified this judgment of hail, fire, and blood being thrown to the earth. Because of this, one-third of the earth was burned up, along with one-third of the trees, and all the green grass was burned up.

Stop to consider this. There is no more green grass around any longer. It's all gone, as are one-third of the trees that had existed on the earth up to that point. That is quite a lot of acreage! It will have a devastating effect on humanity, not to mention animals.

For all their bluster, pride, conceit, and seemingly unstoppable power, the globalists who have been attempting to bring about a one-world system (economic, religious, and social) cannot control everything. God has his say and He takes charge of many of the resources of this earth throughout the Tribulation period to prove to these elitists that they control nothing! They are powerless to keep God from doing whatever He will to His Creation and He reminds them of that fact repeatedly.

The grass, by the way, likely grows again because we see it later in Revelation. But grass will easily replenish itself after forest fires, one of the first things to grow back. We do not know how much time passes between each judgment so there could be time enough for grass to grow in only a few weeks or a month's time.

The 2nd Trumpet Judgment is *"something like a great mountain burning with fire was thrown into the sea; and a third of the sea became blood, and a third of the creatures which were in the sea and had life, died; and a third of the ships were destroyed"* (Revelation 8:8-9).

The words "something like" is John's way of saying that while it looked like a mountain, he wasn't sure that's what it was at all. John could be referencing a large asteroid or meteor. To John, it looked like a mountain. The damage it causes is instant.

- one-third of the sea becomes blood
- one-third of the creatures die
- one-third of ships are destroyed

So far, with just these two judgments, one-third of the trees are burned up, one-third of the earth destroyed, and all grass is gone.

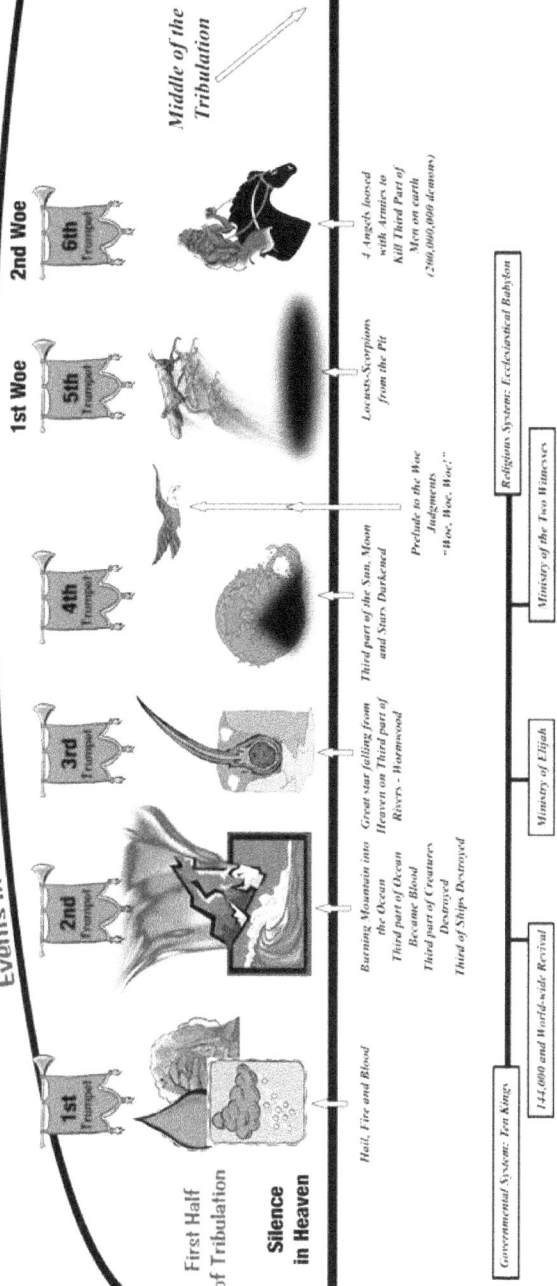

Trumpet Judgments of The Great Tribulation
Revelation 8:1 to 9:21

Events in the Middle of Tribulation. Part 1

Then, one-third of the sea turns to blood (it doesn't say "like blood"), one-third of the creatures in the sea die, and one-third of the ships on the sea are destroyed.

Someone may ask, why and how are the ships destroyed? Put simply, if something large enough to look to John like a mountain falls into the ocean, wouldn't part of the result be seen in tsunamis? Though John doesn't mention it, it may be what he saw and would certainly explain how ships are destroyed. I think it's safe to understand John's meaning in a literal sense here as in most other places in Revelation.

Chapter 26

3rd and 4th Trumpet Judgments

S tarting with the 3rd Trumpet Judgment, we learn the following from Revelation 8:10-11 regarding how the earth and its inhabitants are affected:

> *"The third angel sounded, and a great star fell from heaven, burning like a torch, and it fell on a third of the rivers and on the springs of waters. The name of the star is called Wormwood; and a third of the waters became wormwood, and many men died from the waters, because they were made bitter."*

What is being described by John is likely a meteor or comet. As it enters the earth's atmosphere, it appears to burn like a torch. We've seen this phenomenon with spacecraft coming back to earth from outer space. We know that if the heat shields fail on this reentry, the entire space capsule (and anyone inside) would be destroyed by fire.

That being the case, we know that what John saw was something approaching and entering earth's atmosphere. As it continued its journey through the higher elevations of earth's atmosphere, the fire trail of the object likely grew brighter and longer. The text tells us that this object – whatever it was that John saw – landed on and affected one-third of the rivers and the springs. This tells us that the fresh water supplies of the earth up to one-third will be affected.

Whatever this object is, it manages to poison the waters that it affects. It is called "wormwood" because wormwood, during John's day, was a plant that made water taste very brackish. Drinking enough of it would make one sick. The word "wormwood" literally means "bitter" and the text tells us that *"many men died from the waters, because they were made bitter."* This simply means that whatever toxin this falling star brings to earth, it imperils one-third of the fresh water system enough that drinking it becomes fatal for many.

Thomas Constable notes that *"[wormwood] was the name of a bitter herb that was fatally poisonous to some people and was a symbol of divine punishment (Jeremiah 9:15; Jeremiah 23:15; Lamentations 3:15; Lamentations 3:19; Amos 5:7)."* He also points out that it should remind us of the judgment that God poured out on Israel in the wilderness (Exodus 15).[63]

Following the 3rd Trumpet Judgment, the 4th Trumpet occurs, as highlighted in Revelation 8:12.

> *"The fourth angel sounded, and a third of the sun and a third of the moon and a third of the stars were struck, so that a third of them would be darkened and the day*

---

[63] Thomas Constable, Notes on Revelation, p 92

would not shine for a third of it, and the night in the same way."

Many judgments that occur during the Tribulation period have an effect on one-third of the population, one-third of nature, or one-third of something else. Here, with the 4th Trumpet Judgment, the fourth angel sounds and one-third of the sun, moon, and stars are affected. God turns out the lights – at least one-third.

Now please take the time to consider the results of one-third of the sun going dark. Not only will that greatly dim the heavenly lights, but it will also result in a drastic change in the environment, temperature, and weather. You want to know about so-called "climate change"? Here it is, but God is the One who controls it, as He controls all else. I don't think we can really imagine what will transpire because of this 4th judgment.

Constable points out, "*The text seems to imply that God will reduce the intensity of light from these sources by one-third (cf. Matthew 27:45). Perhaps a partial eclipse or pollution in the atmosphere is in view. Such a reduction in light, and consequently temperature, would have a devastating effect on the earth.*"[64]

Generally, I think we are simply reminded of times when we turn the lights off in our homes. It becomes dark, but the temperature doesn't change. However, the sun, of course, is the source of the earth's light and heat. Without it, there would be no life on earth at all. Science has long told us that if the earth were moved off its appointed place in space by only a few degrees or if the moon drew closer to the earth by a few degrees, havoc would likely result. When the sun goes dark by one-third, there will be havoc on the earth, period. It will not only

---

[64] Thomas Constable, Notes on Revelation, p 92

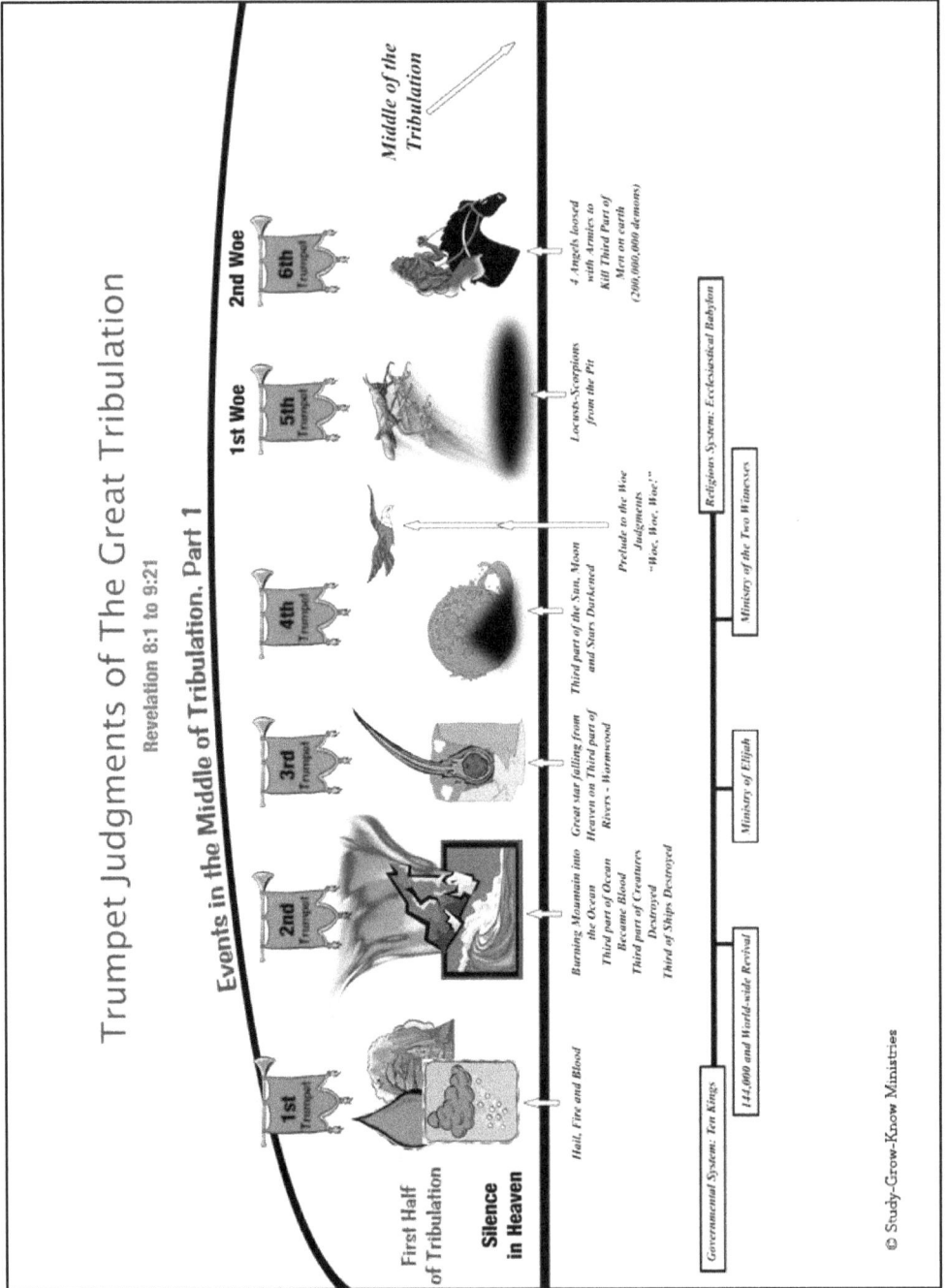

Trumpet Judgments of The Great Tribulation
Revelation 8:1 to 9:21

Events in the Middle of Tribulation, Part 1

First Half of Tribulation

Silence in Heaven

1st Trumpet — Hail, Fire and Blood

2nd Trumpet — Burning Mountain into the Ocean / Third part of Ocean Became Blood / Third part of Creatures Destroyed / Third of Ships Destroyed

3rd Trumpet — Great star falling from Heaven on Third part of Rivers - Wormwood

4th Trumpet — Third part of the Sun, Moon and Stars Darkened

Prelude to the Woe Judgments "Woe, Woe, Woe!"

1st Woe — 5th Trumpet — Locusts-Scorpions from the Pit

2nd Woe — 6th Trumpet — 4 Angels loosed with Armies to Kill Third Part of Men on earth (200,000,000 demons)

Middle of the Tribulation

Governmental System: Ten Kings

144,000 and World-wide Revival

Ministry of Elijah

Ministry of the Two Witnesses

Religious System: Ecclesiastical Babylon

© Study-Grow-Know Ministries

be much darker (even during the day) when this happens, but other things will be affected.

John then tells us what he sees next in Revelation 8:13.

> *"Then I looked, and I heard an eagle flying in midheaven, saying with a loud voice, 'Woe, woe, woe to those who dwell on the earth, because of the remaining blasts of the trumpet of the three angels who are about to sound!'"*

An eagle flies through the heavens and announces the coming three woes along with the remaining Trumpet Judgments. The woes themselves are especially terrible because the target of each of them is the people on the earth.

It would be very good for each person to take some time to study these passages and focus on their reality. We don't spend enough time doing that these days, but we spend a ton of time using our smart phones, playing video games, and being on the computer. Our attention span has grown much shorter (not by accident either) and it is more difficult for us to be and remain focused on the things of God.

Chapter 27

5th Trumpet Judgment

I n our last chapter, we covered the 3rd and 4th Trumpet Judgments of Revelation 8, as well as the first "woe" of three woes. This 1st Woe (Revelation 8:13) was signaled by the flight of an eagle across the heavens and it is a precursor to the sounding of the 5th Trumpet Judgment. This woe is a warning to all inhabitants of the earth that more terrible things are going to start to occur.

The next judgment happens following the sounding of the 5th Trumpet. This is a very interesting judgment. Let's look at the text in parts, first in Revelation 9:1-3.

> "*The fifth angel sounded his trumpet, and I saw a star that had fallen from the sky to the earth. The star was*

*given the key to the shaft of the Abyss. When he opened
the Abyss, smoke rose from it like the smoke from a gigantic furnace. The sun and sky were darkened by the
smoke from the Abyss. And out of the smoke locusts came
down on the earth and were given power like that of
scorpions of the earth."*

Picture the scene. The 5th Trumpet sounds and John sees a "star that
had fallen from the sky to the earth." This "star" was given the key to
open up the gateway to the Abyss. The "star" referenced here cannot
be a physical planet of the heavenly realm that merely reflects the
sun's light, as this star has intelligence.

The star is very likely some angelic being. We cannot be certain who
the star is but it's possible the star is Satan or some high-ranking unfallen angel.

The phrase *"had fallen from the sky…"* may not refer to the condition
of the star (angel) at all, as though one of the fallen angels, but may
simply be referencing a trajectory that the angel took from the sky to
the entrance to the Abyss. If the star is not a fallen angel, then it could
very well be an unfallen angel simply fulfilling the direction of God.

I agree with numerous scholars that this particular star is an unfallen
angel, who follows God's directives to a "T." His job is to open the entrance to the pit or Abyss to release "locusts" from that holding cell,
so to speak.

Note in verses 2 and 3 the following description:

*"When he opened the Abyss, smoke rose from it like the
smoke from a gigantic furnace. The sun and sky were
darkened by the smoke from the Abyss."*

The "Locust" of Revelation 9?

When this angel opens the entrance to the Abyss, the first thing John sees is smoke "like" or "as if" it was the smoke from a gigantic furnace. That simply means that it reminded John of smoke from a huge furnace, not that there actually was a gigantic furnace there. We can all picture thick, dark plumes of smoke coming from large smokestacks. This is what John saw. In fact, the smoke was so thick that both the sun and the sky were darkened because of it.

Take the time to picture this for your own sake. It's obviously daytime, yet the amount and darkness of the smoke makes it feel as though it is nighttime. If you were alive at this point and all of a sudden, the sky and sun turned dark, would you not become afraid? I think most people would because such a drastic turn from full day to something that appears to be night is not a normal situation. The suddenness of it all would make all the people of the earth take note and have reason to fear.

Revelation 9:3 tells us what happens next.

> *"And out of the smoke locusts came down on the earth*
> *and were given power like that of scorpions of the earth."*

The smoke is very thick and dark and while people are very likely looking up at the sky, they begin to see some type of creatures coming out of the smoke. Talk about an invasion! This is what horror movies are made of. I've created a graphic of what the Bible de-scribes that these "locusts" look like. Clearly, these creatures are be-yond description, but John did the best he could. It's not what they look like so much as what they accomplish.

At this point, the people are likely not aware that these supernatural creatures have specific abilities, but John tells us that they are given power similar to scorpions of the earth.

There are thousands of species of scorpions throughout the world, but only 30 of them have toxins that are dangerous to human beings. In the southern part of the United States, it is not uncommon to find them in your home. The sting can be painful. The scorpion in the im-age is reared up and ready to fight if necessary to save its own life from predators. Scorpions are aggressive and generally don't back down. These scorpions described in Scripture will be unique from other normal scorpions that currently exist on earth.

Revelation 9:4 tells us more about these scorpions:

> *"They were told not to harm the grass of the earth or any plant or tree, but only those people who did not have the seal of God on their foreheads."*

These cannot be normal, run-of-the-mill scorpions because these have the ability to distinguish between grass, plants, trees, and hu-mans. In fact, they are told to only go after humans who do not have God's seal on their forehead. It is this type of information that makes me believe these scorpions are not scorpions, but *demons* that may resemble aspects of scorpions.

Revelation 9:5 informs us that *"They were not allowed to kill them but only to torture them for five months. And the agony they suffered was like that of the sting of a scorpion when it strikes."* These particular "scorpions" (demons) could not kill anyone but were simply ordered to torture people with their stings during a window of time equal to five months. There is no reason to believe that the "five months" here ultimately means something else. It likely means five months.

We are also told that the sting from these creatures causes great agony, but not death. The next verse – Revelation 9:6 – explains even more. "*During those days people will seek death but will not find it; they will long to die, but death will elude them.*"

Try to imagine that. The pain is so intense that people will want to die, but will be unable to commit suicide. God wants them to endure the pain. He wants them to wake up to their plight. He wants them to understand what eternity without Him will be like. He wants no one to perish and takes no delight in the death of sinners (cf. Ezekiel 18:32), but He is going to use extreme measures in an attempt to wake people up from the sin-laden slumber. He wants them saved, not to die in their sin.

Do you know anyone who does not know Jesus as Savior/Lord? If they are alive during the coming Tribulation and do not know Jesus, this is what they may experience. Christians need to do all that's possible to warn people of the coming judgments. It's our job – the Great Commission.

Chapter 28

Description of Locusts

I n our previous chapter, we spoke mainly about the first aspect of the 5th Trumpet. This is where the angel blows his trumpet and the 5th judgment begins. A "star" or angel falls to earth and is given the key to the Abyss where, after he opens the door, dark smoke billows up and legions of locusts are released onto the earth. This is all recorded for us in Revelation 9:1ff.

We ended our last chapter with Revelation 9:6 where it tells us that the sting from these creatures will be *like* the sting of a scorpion. Clearly, if they were actual scorpions, their sting would not be "like" a scorpion's sting. It would *be* a scorpion's sting! Nonetheless, the sting will be so bad that people will want to die but death will elude them. They won't even be able to take their own lives, apparently.

We're going to pick it up from Revelation 9:7-10, which provides a detailed description of these creatures.

> *"The appearance of the locusts was like horses prepared for battle; and on their heads appeared to be crowns like gold, and their faces were like the faces of men. They had hair like the hair of women, and their teeth were like the teeth of lions. They had breastplates like breastplates of iron; and the sound of their wings was like the sound of chariots, of many horses rushing to battle. They have tails like scorpions, and stings; and in their tails is their power to hurt men for five months."*

The job of these ugly, fearsome creatures is to hurt or torment people for five months. They have limitations. They are not allowed to kill anyone, but are allowed and encouraged to inflict severe physical pain. They are not allowed to hurt the grass, plants, or trees either (cf. 9:4-5). Notice all the comparisons. Locusts eat trees, grass, and plants. These creatures are actually *not* locusts, but to John, they resembled locusts.

Their sole focus is on terrifying and inflicting injury on people. As I said in my last chapter, God is trying to get people's attention and He is using drastic measures to do so. Pain and terror weakens people, who often then cry out for release or solace. It is often when people are at their lowest that they begin to turn to God. Will it happen here? We'll see if God's Word answers that question.

In the meantime, the above verses give us a picture of these creatures. Notice that the head of a locust looks similar in some ways to the head of a horse, but these also have something that reminded John of a *crown* on their heads.

A horse's head is long with its eyes at the top. Locusts share the same trait. The text says that *"The appearance of the locusts was LIKE..."* and that means not that the locusts had horses' heads, but that their heads were *reminiscent* of horses' heads.

Horses that are prepared for battle are often dressed with armor and are very alert to what is happening around them. They are prepared to follow their leader anywhere. So it is with these locusts. They have been released from the Abyss and they know they have a job to do, a job from which they do not shrink.

The book of Joel also speaks of swarms of locusts that attack in the latter days or as the day of the Lord approaches (Joel 1:15). Joel 2:4 also uses descriptive language to describe these locusts.

> *"Their appearance is like the appearance of horses; And like war horses, so they run."*

In Joel 2:11 we learn that this army of locusts is the Lord's army.

> *"The Lord utters His voice before His army; Surely His camp is very great,*

> *"For strong is he who carries out His word. The day of the Lord is indeed great and very awesome, And who can endure it?"*

This army of supernatural creatures that resemble and act like locusts is an army under the direct control of God Himself.

Notice though that these locusts, as described in Scripture, had faces like men's faces and hair like women's hair. Their teeth did not remind John of human teeth but of teeth in a lion's mouth. They wore breastplates of iron and they had wings, which all told made tremendous noise when they flew. Finally, these creatures had something in their tails (like scorpions) that allowed them to hurt men for five months.

Some people like to believe that what John is describing in this part of Revelation is modern-day military hardware: planes, helicopters, and things of that nature. The problem with this is that these creatures seem to be imbued with the ability to *reason* and to distinguish between human beings and foliage and those who were marked for God those who were not. The fact that they were told not to hurt the plants, grass, or trees and to simply focus on humans is also a point in favor of the fact that they are intelligent beings, not hardware that is programmed, which can make mistakes, depending on the programming software.

In my mind, these are supernatural beings that would certainly look weird to us because they do not exist in our realm. I doubt we can imagine what all the various creatures look like that reside in the spiritual realm. Even some of the angels that are described by Ezekiel and others are too strange for us to picture. But because we cannot adequately picture something does not mean that it can't be a living being. The many angels in the Bible that are described to us often looked like men; however, certain cherubim or seraphim descriptions appear very strange to us.

Revelation 9:11 tells us, "*They have as king over them, the angel of the abyss; his name in Hebrew is Abaddon, and in the Greek he has the name Apollyon.*" This king could very well be Satan himself. Though he is in charge of this group, it is clear that when God steps in to control them for His purposes, they become His.

This 5th Trumpet is also the 1st Woe, the one that the eagle spoke of in Revelation 8. Next chapter, we will deal with the 6th Trumpet Judgment, which is also the 2nd Woe. Following this, we will get into the final set of seven judgments, the Seven Bowls.

Chapter 29

6th Trumpet Judgment

I n our last chapter, we discussed the locust-like creatures who rise from the Abyss to inflict terrible pain on humankind for five months. The creatures are not allowed to kill, nor are they allowed to damage the grass, trees, or bushes (which normal locusts would do). Their focus is on those who are not sealed with God's seal. The pain will be so intense that people will wish to die, but even death will elude them.

It sounds bad if you ask me. Revelation 9:12 refers to this judgment as the 1st Woe. There are still two other woes that those of earth must endure.

Revelation 9:13 begins describing the next phase of the Tribulation, the 6th Trumpet that brings the army of the east into view.

> *"13 Then the sixth angel sounded, and I heard a voice from the four horns of the golden altar which is before God, 14 one saying to the sixth angel who had the trumpet, 'Release the four angels who are bound at the great river Euphrates.' 15 And the four angels, who had been prepared for the hour and day and month and year, were released, so that they would kill a third of mankind. 16 The number of the armies of the horsemen was two hundred million; I heard the number of them."*

It is incredible to think that all of the things described in this book (related to the final upcoming seven years of human history, prior to the return of Jesus and His 1,000 year reign) will happen. If people would simply take the time to learn what God's Word says and concentrate on these facts, more would likely turn to Him in true repentance.

Unfortunately, as we see in numerous places throughout the Tribulation, even amid all of these terrible judgments, people refuse to repent. They refuse to recognize their own sinfulness, which would allow them to turn to Him. Instead, they soldier on, devoted to their own arrogance and eventual destruction. It's not as though they will be able to claim they were not warned either.

These Seals, Trumpets, and Bowls are sent by God for the deliberate purpose of purifying Israel and for drawing the world to Him. The absolute arrogance that is on display by people who live during the Tribulation is astounding. We need to remember that God allowed the apostle John to see the future as it was going to unfold. He saw it, just as Isaiah saw what God revealed to him. These were not dreams. They were true visions of events that would take place.

In this 6th Trumpet, four angels are released. These angels are "bound" at the Euphrates. Since they are bound – literally "in chains" – we know that they cannot be unfallen angels (2 Pet. 2:4; Jude 6).

They are undoubtedly fallen angels who are objects of God's wrath and because of that He uses them for this purpose. In fact, the text tells us that these four particular angels *"had been prepared for the hour and day and month and year...."*

At the exact moment in time specified by God, these four "bound" angels were released in order to kill one-third of all mankind. The four angels will marshal a force totaling 200 million individuals. John even states that he heard the number itself. He wasn't approximating based on what he saw. He saw and heard the exact number that makes up this deathly army. Two hundred million individuals appear to march across the earth taking one-third of mankind from the face of the earth through death. None of this should be taken metaphorically. It appears to be very literal.

Years ago, when I first began studying the subject of the end times, I recall that in certain books, it was taught that this 200-million-man army was made up of Asians from the east. The author would then note that China already had (at that time) an army of 200 million soldiers. It's really a very large number, and if we consider that the total Allied and Axis forces at their peak in World War II totaled about 70 million,[65] it makes it difficult to believe that the 200 million number represents human beings. It is more likely that it represents demons, though it could be a mixture of demons and humans. In the end, we should take the 200 million to be a literal number.

By the time these troops led by these four angels are finished with their task to kill one-third of humans who have rejected God, a total of roughly one-half of the earth's entire population will be gone. Oth-

---

[65] http://www.historynet.com/world-war-ii (04/15/2015)

er judgments have taken one-quarter of the world's population in death since the start of the Tribulation. That one-quarter added to the one-third gives us a total of roughly one-half. Right now, there are over seven billion people on the earth. After the 6th Trumpet, three and a half billion would remain if the Tribulation were to begin today.

The next portion of Scripture describes these creatures to us.

> *"17 And this is how I saw in the vision the horses and those who sat on them: the riders had breastplates the color of fire and of hyacinth and of brimstone; and the heads of the horses are like the heads of lions; and out of their mouths proceed fire and smoke and brimstone. 18 A third of mankind was killed by these three plagues, by the fire and the smoke and the brimstone which proceeded out of their mouths. 19 For the power of the horses is in their mouths and in their tails; for their tails are like serpents and have heads, and with them they do harm."*

After reading this section of Scripture, it is fairly easy to understand these 200 million as being of supernatural origin. John is not describing human beings here, is he? He is describing creatures that carry riders. These creatures have heads like lions instead of heads like horses. These lions are able to shoot fire, smoke, and brimstone. They almost sound like dragons. The "horses" not only have power in their mouths, but in their tails as well. Their tails are like snakes, including heads. These creatures have the ability to kill what is in front of them as well as what is behind them.

While it is certainly possible that the riders of these creatures will be human it is also possible that John's figurative language here is just that – figurative. The real point, though, is that this army of 200 million will kill one-third of the world's population. That is the 6th Trumpet.

Chapter 30

Revelation 10

L ast chapter, we covered the 6th Trumpet of Revelation. We're going toward the 7th Trumpet, but before we do, we need to discuss the contents of Revelation 10 as well as the Two Witnesses in Revelation 11.

You'll recall that with the blowing of the 6th Trumpet, four angels who had been bound at the Euphrates River until just that specific time were released. These angels were given the task of killing one-third of mankind with an army of 200 million soldiers. We spent some time discussing the possibilities regarding the makeup of these soldiers, whether they were human or demonic. The description of the soldiers in Revelation 9:17-19 tends to point toward these soldiers being supernatural (demonic) as opposed to human. However, we won't know for certain until that event happens.

Let's also not forget that even after the 6th Trumpet does its work, we read in the last few verses of Revelation 9:20-21 that no one repented.

> *"The rest of mankind, who were not killed by these plagues, did not repent of the works of their hands, so as not to worship demons, and the idols of gold and of silver and of brass and of stone and of wood, which can neither see nor hear nor walk; and they did not repent of their murders nor of their sorceries nor of their immorality nor of their thefts."*

That should amaze people. Considering how brutal the Trumpet Judgments have been so far, you would think that people would be on their knees pleading for mercy. Nope, not the arrogant people of earth. Repentance is not something to which they will stoop.

Revelation 10 is a relatively short chapter in which we see a bit of pageantry occurring in the heavenly realms. In my opinion, the first verse tells me that this angel is not the Lord Jesus Christ. I realize that others disagree with that assessment and the point is not to argue over it.

> *"I saw another strong angel coming down out of heaven, clothed with a cloud; and the rainbow was upon his head, and his face was like the sun, and his feet like pillars of fire..."* (Revelation 10:1)

The fact that the text says *"I saw another strong angel coming down out of heaven"* tells me that this is exactly what John saw. He saw "another angel." I believe he would have known instantly if this was Jesus, but John describes this being as "another" angel. I think it would be impossible to mistake Jesus for an angel or an angel for Jesus.

The angel has a book (v. 2) which is open. The angel then places his left foot on the land and his right on the sea. When he spoke, it was like the roar of a lion. In response, the seven peals of thunder uttered their voices. John was about to write down what the thunders said, but he was told not to do so. Following this, the strong angel with the little book swears by Him who lives forever and who created all things. We know according to Hebrews 1 and Colossians 1 that Jesus is the Creator of all things.

This all happens just before the blowing of the 7th Trumpet. John is then told to take the "little book" and swallow it. The book tasted sweet to John but as soon as he swallowed it, it was sour in his stomach.

This is often the case with prophecy regarding the end times. There is sweetness in knowing the end result; however, to get to that point is often painful and filled with sorrow. All of the coming judgments are filled with pain and sorrow, yet we know who wins the final battle.

Chapter 31

Two Witnesses of Revelation 11

I n this interlude of Revelation 11, we are introduced to the Two Witnesses. There, we not only learn about these two men, but we learn more about the Temple area in Jerusalem. The chapter begins by highlighting the fact that John is given a measuring rod and is told to measure the Temple and altar.

> *"1 Then there was given me a measuring rod like a staff; and someone said, 'Get up and measure the temple of God and the altar, and those who worship in it. 2 Leave out the court which is outside the temple and do not measure it, for it has been given to the nations; and they will tread underfoot the holy city for forty-two months'"* (Revelation 11:1-2).

The above verses tell us several important things. John is told to measure the area where people worship God. This excludes the outer court area, outside the Temple proper. Notice John is told that these areas have been given over to the nations for a period of forty-two (42) months. Forty-two months is three and a half years (3 1/2) and is the time of the first portion of the Seven-Year Tribulation period, which at its end will lead up to the physical return of Jesus.

We can see during the first portion of the Tribulation that the Gentile nations will continue to trample the outer court area, though it also appears that the inside of the Temple itself will be protected. This trampling began way back with Nebuchadnezzar's Babylonian Kingdom. That was the start of the "Times of the Gentiles" and it will not conclude until Jesus returns.

From here, we are directed to the Two Witnesses (Revelation 11:3-6). God does not tell us who they are, and because of that, opinions run the gamut. Apparently, it isn't important that we know, otherwise God would have told us. There are actually people alive now who claim they are the Two Witnesses spoken of here:

> "'And I will grant authority to my two witnesses, and they will prophesy for twelve hundred and sixty days, clothed in sackcloth.' These are the two olive trees and the two lampstands that stand before the Lord of the earth. And if anyone wants to harm them, fire flows out of their mouth and devours their enemies; so if anyone wants to harm them, he must be killed in this way. These have the power to shut up the sky, so that rain will not fall during the days of their prophesying; and they have power over the waters to turn them into blood, and to strike the earth with every plague, as often as they desire."

God grants authority to His Two Witnesses to do several things in order to call people to repentance and to protect the Temple area:

- They will prophesy for 1,260 days. This figure is equal to 42 months, which is equal to 3 1/2 years (1 year on God's calendar equaling 360 days, not 365 days). This most likely refers to the Great Tribulation or the last 3 1/2 years of the Seven-Year Tribulation (cf. Matthew 24)
- Prophecy includes teaching, and in their case, they will teach people the truth (whether the people listen or not)
- They will be dressed in sackcloth, signifying the need for repentance by the people who hear them because of approaching judgment
- They are called "the two olive trees" and "the two lampstands" who stand before the Lord
- These two individuals will literally represent the Living God on earth during this time
- There are Two Witnesses because in the Hebrew Bible (Old Testament) valid testimony required two witnesses
- They are "lampstands" signifying they will be empowered by the Holy Spirit to be God's representative light on the earth
- The Witnesses will have the power to protect themselves from anyone who wishes to harm them
- They may use fire from their mouths to literally devour enemies, or it may also mean that they will be able to call down fire from heaven to kill enemies as Elijah did (2 Kings 1:10-14)The Witnesses also have the ability to keep it from raining for as long as they would like
- The Witnesses will be able to turn water into blood (not "like" blood, but actual blood)
- The Witnesses will have the power to use any plague they desire on the earth and its residents whenever they want to do so
- Since the Witnesses' ministry expands to the final 3 1/2 years of the Great Tribulation, they may be the ones who also assist in the final Trumpet and Bowl Judgments as well

Once these Two Witnesses have completed their mission and ministry, their protective power will be held at bay and the "beast" from the Abyss will be allowed to kill them.

> *"When they have finished their testimony, the beast that comes up out of the abyss will make war with them, and overcome them and kill them. And their dead bodies will lie in the street of the great city which mystically is called Sodom and Egypt, where also their Lord was crucified. Those from the peoples and tribes and tongues and nations will look at their dead bodies for three and a half days, and will not permit their dead bodies to be laid in a tomb. And those who dwell on the earth will rejoice over them and celebrate; and they will send gifts to one another, because these two prophets tormented those who dwell on the earth"* (Revelation 11:7-10).

This beast, of course, is the Antichrist, who is completely indwelt by Satan himself. Not only does the Antichrist kill these Two Witnesses, but he prohibits anyone from burying them. He wants their dead bodies to remain in the streets for three and a half days. I find verse 10 very interesting. The people are so happy about the deaths of these Two Witnesses that they have a worldwide celebration, even sending gifts to one another. Obviously, most people did not heed the message at all in spite of the terrible things that the Two Witnesses brought upon the earth. The people were simply very glad they were finally gone.

By the way, this situation with the Two Witnesses is actually what the Scriptures call the *"second woe"* (cf. Revelation 11:14). This 2nd Woe is the last event that takes place prior to the blowing of the 7th Trumpet Judgment.

> *"But after the three and a half days, the breath of life from God came into them, and they stood on their feet;*

and great fear fell upon those who were watching them. And they heard a loud voice from heaven saying to them, 'Come up here.' Then they went up into heaven in the cloud, and their enemies watched them. And in that hour there was a great earthquake, and a tenth of the city fell; seven thousand people were killed in the earthquake, and the rest were terrified and gave glory to the God of heaven" (Revelation 11:11-13).

The Two Witnesses are resurrected and received into the heavens. Because of this, people are terrified, as anyone would be. That very hour, a tremendous earthquake occurs, leaving one-tenth of the city (Jerusalem) in ruins and 7,000 dead. The remainder of people were so terrified that they gave glory to God. However, it is short-lived.

Chapter 32

7ᵗʰ Trumpet Judgment

R evelation 11:15-19 is the text from Scripture that introduces
the 7th Trumpet Judgment to us.

*"Then the seventh angel sounded; and there were loud
voices in heaven, saying,*

*"'The kingdom of the world has become the kingdom of
our Lord and of His Christ; and He will reign forever and
ever.' And the twenty-four elders, who sit on their thrones
before God, fell on their faces and worshiped God, saying,*

*"'We give You thanks, O Lord God, the Almighty, who are
and who were, because You have taken Your great power
and have begun to reign. And the nations were enraged,
and Your wrath came, and the time came for the dead to
be judged, and the time to reward Your bond-servants the
prophets and the saints and those who fear Your name,
the small and the great, and to destroy those who destroy
the earth.'*

*"And the temple of God which is in heaven was opened;
and the ark of His covenant appeared in His temple, and
there were flashes of lightning and sounds and peals of
thunder and an earthquake and a great hailstorm."*

Obviously, the text above is the prelude to the blowing of the 7th
Trumpet that releases the Bowl Judgments. After the ministry of the
Two Witnesses on earth is complete, stretching over 1,260 days, or 3
1/2 years, they are killed. Three and a half days later they are resurrected and called back to heaven. At that point, a tremendously de-
structive earthquake occurs, destroying one-tenth of Jerusalem and
killing 7,000 people. Those remaining are so afraid they become
temporarily humbled and give glory to God.

Now, an angel blows the 7th Trumpet and several things happen. In
essence, because we are nearing the end of the Tribulation/Great
Tribulation, all things are as good as done. The kingdom of the world
(Satan's kingdom) has changed ownership, permanently, and has become the Lord's. God in Christ is now getting ready to reign forever
and ever. He does so first by reigning 1,000 years on earth in the Millennial Kingdom from His father David's throne. Once that is completed, His reign continues...*forever*. There is no break from His complete and total reign once He begins to physically reign.

The remainder of the text reflects the praise from the mouths of angels, elders, and other creatures for God and His infinite reign, which

will never again be challenged by anyone. When these complete their praise, verse 19 tells us that God's Temple – the one in heaven – is opened and the Ark of His covenant is seen. Flashes of lightning and peals of thunder occur along with an earthquake and a hailstorm.

Much of the picture here reminds us of the setting of Mt. Sinai when Moses was taken to the top of the mountain and the mountain shook because of God's voice when He spoke to the people. This is all in preparation for God to speak to the earth once again through God the Son as He prepares to return to earth as Supreme Victor.

Chapter 33

1st, 2nd, 3rd Bowl Judgments

A t this point, we are going to skip over a few chapters of Revelation to get to chapter *16*. Here, we pick up the continuation of judgments from God Himself. Here, we see the contents of the Seven Bowls of judgment.

Bowl 1 – Loathsome Sores (Revelation 16:1-2)
This bowl creates "loathsome sores" over the entire bodies of people on the earth.

> *"Then I heard a loud voice from the temple, saying to the seven angels, 'Go and pour out on the earth the seven bowls of the wrath of God.'*

"So the first angel went and poured out his bowl on the earth; and it became a loathsome and malignant sore on the people who had the mark of the beast and who worshiped his image."

Whether the angels pour out all the individual bowls of God's wrath at once or in succession, we really don't know. God simply tells the angels to pour out the contents of the bowls and the bowls here are clearly labeled "the wrath of God." This is not Satan's wrath. It is not people's wrath. It is God's wrath directed to the people on the earth for their lack of surrender to His will.

The text tells us that the first angel poured out the contents of his bowl of God's wrath and immediately people began experiencing loathsome and malignant sores. This happened to anyone who had taken the mark of the beast (whatever that turns out to be). God is done with these people. They are not protected from His wrath and will now experience it as a precursor of what is to come.

Bowl 2 – Salt Water to Blood (Revelation 16:3)

"The second angel poured out his bowl into the sea, and it became blood like that of a dead man; and every living thing in the sea died."

This is massive. The contents of the 2nd Bowl of God's wrath were poured out into the sea and the sea became blood. Because of that, everything in the sea that was alive died. There are no living creatures left because of this bowl of God's wrath! Imagine the stench. Imagine that any desalinization systems that turned sea water into potable water would no longer work! Imagine what that would do to the world and its population.

Bowl 3 – Rivers and Water Springs to Blood (Revelation 16:4-7)

"Then the third angel poured out his bowl into the rivers and the springs of waters; and they became blood. And I heard the

angel of the waters saying, 'Righteous are You, who are and who were, O Holy One, because You judged these things; for they poured out the blood of saints and prophets, and You have given them blood to drink. They deserve it.' And I heard the altar saying, 'Yes, O Lord God, the Almighty, true and righteous are Your judgments.'"

The 3rd Bowl of God's wrath turns the rivers and springs of waters to blood. Notice it does not say "like" blood, but they "became blood." More stench, more death, and now a complete lack of potable drinking water. The addendum to this is that in essence, this judgment is payback for all the blood of the saints and prophets that the world has shed since the beginning. The world killed millions of believers, and now, the only thing they will have to drink is the blood that represents the lives of these saints.

The Great Tribulation is not over yet. There are still several more bowls yet to be poured out onto the earth before it's done. We will pick it up with the 4th Bowl of God's Wrath next!

Chapter 34

More Bowl Judgments

I would like to offer a reminder that *all* the judgments – Seven Seals, Seven Trumpets, and Seven Bowls – stem from the action that occurs in the throne room. The Lamb of God Himself – Jesus Christ – *controls* the timing and release of each of these judgments. Together, all 21 judgments are from God. They are not created by man, nor are they from Satan. They are from God, period. They represent God's wrath on man and this earth, not man's wrath.

Before we get further into this, I would also like to recommend a book I've written on Revelation,[66] available through Amazon. It is not

---

[66] To order, go to Amazon.com and search for *End of the Ages*, by Fred DeRuvo

as detailed as some other commentaries, but it makes a good primer on the subject at just over 400 pages.

Another book (or set of two volumes actually) is one I cannot recommend enough. It's written by Dr. Tony Garland, a man who spent most of his life as a Covenant/Reformed Theologian and says he woke to the error of that system to embrace a far more conservative and literal approach. Today, he is a PreTrib Rapture believer and his books are extremely detailed, going into the original languages. They are "*A Testimony of Jesus Christ*," volumes one and two. However, if purchased via Kindle, it is one complete volume. Well worth having for the serious Bible student.

I will also note this. There are several ways to interpret Scripture, but only one of them is the correct way. There is the allegorical way of understanding the Word of God, but in that case, unless the particular text is allegorical (a figure of speech, a metaphor, etc.) it does serious damage to Scripture to take the Bible allegorically.

Yet, many people automatically do this when it comes to the many prophetic passages in the Bible. They see the symbolism, etc., and automatically take it as *allegorical*.

Fine

for

Littering

Another way of understanding Scripture is to interpret the Bible *literally*. Unfortunately, though, many confuse literal with *literalistic*.

As an example, look at the image of the sign. It says "Fine for Littering." Taking it literally, we know that it means "do not litter, and if caught, a fee/tax will be issued."

However, for the person who is on the Autism Spectrum, that same sign might actually mean "it's okay to litter here" to *them*. In these examples, we see that one person understood the meaning literally, while the second person understood the meaning *literalistically*. There is only one correct way to interpret the sign though.

It's the same with figures of speech that we use in normal conversation. Overhearing someone say, "*I'm so hungry I could eat a horse!*" is not taken to mean that the person is actually going to or wants to eat a horse. We understand the meaning to simply be a figurative way of stating how hungry that person is now.

This is why when we come to certain passages in Scripture that reference the "dragon" or "beast" as seen in Revelation 13, where there are actually two beasts indicated, we do not understand Scripture to be saying that what we will see in the future are actual beasts that rise from the sea or land as if living sea monsters. We understand the term "beasts" to reference kingdoms, and to interpret Scripture in such a way is actually taking it literally.

Of course, this is because we allow Scripture to interpret Scripture. To believe that the Bible is referencing two real beasts – as living monsters – is to take the Bible literalistically. This is something we should avoid doing. Remember, the goal is to understand God's Word literally or as God intended it when He wrote it through holy men of old. We know that the reference to the beasts in Revelation goes all the way back to Daniel 2 and other portions of Daniel. In those cases, we know for a fact that the parts of the statue and the beasts connected to it refer to specific human empires and the characteristics of those empires.

The 4th Bowl Judgment

This is why books like Revelation are confusing to people. Many do not see the connections from Revelation to Daniel, Ezekiel, or other books of the Bible. We fail to understand that God wrote the entire Bible using roughly 40 human authors over a period of roughly 1,600 to 2,000 years. Yet, it was God who oversaw its writings. It is best to see God's Word in those terms because it allows us to avoid a great many mistakes.

As we move through Revelation, we come to the 4th and 5th Bowl Judgments in fairly quick succession in Revelation 16:8-11.

> *"The fourth angel poured out his bowl upon the sun, and it was given to it to scorch men with fire. Men were scorched with fierce heat; and they blasphemed the name of God who has the power over these plagues, and they did not repent so as to give Him glory.*

> *"Then the fifth angel poured out his bowl on the throne of the beast, and his kingdom became darkened; and they gnawed their tongues because of pain, and they blasphemed the God of heaven because of their pains and their sores; and they did not repent of their deeds."*

For those who will doubt God's integrity, veracity, or intent, He continues to pour out bowls of His wrath on the earth. In the 4th Bowl Judgment, we see that somehow, the sun becomes hotter and scorches men with fire. While the 4th Trumpet darkened the sun, it is interesting to note that the 4th Bowl brightens the sun, or increases the sun's intensity.

There is a definite article before "men" in the Greek text. The men in view are evidently the people who have the mark of the beast and who worship him (v. 2). The faithful will apparently escape this judgment. Similarly, the Israelites escaped some of the plagues on Egypt.[67]

Note that even in the midst of these horrible situations, those who never received the mark of the beast – the faithful – will avoid this judgment by God's grace and mercy. By the way, along those lines, I

---

[67] http://soniclight.com/constable/notes/pdf/revelation.pdf

find it fascinating today that there are many Christians who bemoan the idea of the PreTrib Rapture. They sneer at those who believe it – something they consider apostate – and I've even read recently one individual who believes this particular doctrine is part of the deception of the new world order. Through their arrogance, they believe that the Church – Christ's Bride – must go through a purification found within the Tribulation. Not only do I not see this in Scripture, but one might almost say that this belief is a type of works. It tends to negate the cross work of Jesus upon whom God the Father's wrath was poured out so that His children – those who trust in Jesus as Savior/Lord – will never have to experience it in this life or the next.

Notice the reaction of those whose flesh is scorched due to the increased intensity of the sun. They blaspheme God. They don't submit to Him. They don't humble themselves. As Pharaoh of old did, they harden their hearts, dig in their heels, and continue to hate God. Repentance for them is not even in the picture. Hatred of God and His ways are all that matter to them.

The 5ᵗʰ Bowl Judgment

The 5ᵗʰ Bowl Judgment is poured out on the throne of the beast, which directly impacts his earthly kingdom. This again is God's wrath. The lights will go out, just as they did during the days before the Exodus in Egypt when the Egyptians experienced utter darkness but the Israelites did not (cf. Exodus 10:21-22).

Numerous individuals have chosen to take this section allegorically when there is absolutely no need to do so unless they also want to take the plague of Exodus 10:21-22 allegorically as well. When Jesus died on the cross, was that darkness literal or figurative? It can't be one way in Scripture and then another way in a different part unless there is something specific that tells us it is *not* to be taken literally, but should be taken allegorically or metaphorically. But remember, there must be a good reason to take the text that way.

We do not know why this darkness causes physical pain for those on earth. We can get a glimpse from the 9th plague visited upon the Egyptians and the resulting confusion and fear, but Scripture is essentially silent. We know that in spite of their pain and sores (possibly from the 4th Bowl Judgment), they continue to blaspheme God.

Chapter 35

6th Bowl Judgment

Previously, we highlighted the 4th and 5th Bowl Judgments of Revelation 16 that lead up to the Battle of Armageddon. The 6th Bowl Judgment is more of a political judgment in preparation for this battle, though it is obviously a physical judgment as well (Revelation 16:12).

> *"The sixth angel poured out his bowl on the great river,*
> *the Euphrates; and its water was dried up, so that the*
> *way would be prepared for the kings from the east."*

Clearly, the reason that the Euphrates River becomes dry is to benefit the kings of the east as they begin to gather their armies for the upcoming war. In that sense, this judgment is to prepare the way for the war that will take place. Dr. Thomas Constable notes:

> "[The Sixth Bowl Judgment] does not inflict a plague on people but serves as a preparation for the final eschatological battle.571 The Euphrates River is the northeastern border of the land God promised to Abraham's descendants (Gen. 15:18; Deut. 1:7; 11:24; Josh. 1:4). The Bible calls the Euphrates River (cf. Gen. 2:14), the eastern border of the Promised Land, the great river; and it calls the Mediterranean Sea, the western border of the Promised Land, the Great Sea."[68]

God specifically dries this river up in order that the kings from the east with their armies can cross into the Megiddo Plain. I see no reason to take this passage in a way other than literally. On numerous occasions, God dried up seas or river beds for His purposes. We see this with the crossing of the Red Sea (Exodus 14), the Jordan River (Joshua 3), Elijah parting the waters of the Jordan River (2 Kings 2), and as Constable notes, Cyrus dried up the river bed by diverting the water in order to conquer Babylon (Jeremiah 50). Again, there is absolutely no reason to interpret this verse in Revelation as a metaphor since there are numerous examples of God drying up river or sea beds in the past.

Revelation 16:13-16 provides us more detail on the future war we know as Armageddon.

> "And I saw coming out of the mouth of the dragon and out of the mouth of the beast and out of the mouth of the false prophet, three unclean spirits like frogs; for they are spirits of demons, performing signs, which go out to the kings of the whole world, to gather them together for the

[68] http://www.soniclight.com/constable/notes/pdf/revelation.pdf, p. 148

war of the great day of God, the Almighty. ('Behold, I am coming like a thief. Blessed is the one who stays awake and keeps his clothes, so that he will not walk about naked and men will not see his shame.'). And they gathered them together to the place which in Hebrew is called Har-Magedon."

The above verses provide more information for us on the details of the 6th Bowl Judgment and its effect on the world, politically. Reference is made to the dragon (known to be Satan), the beast (Antichrist), and the false prophet and the three unclean spirits (like frogs, not actual frogs, reminiscent of one of the plagues God meted out on Egypt) that come out of them. Verse 14 tells us without equivocation that the three unclean spirits that proceed out of their mouths are demons. These particular demons perform the types of signs and wonders that wind up mesmerizing the kings of the world and cause them to gather together for war. This coming war is referred to by John as the "great day of God, the Almighty." Clearly, this is pointing to the fact that this war – Armageddon – will ultimately be a direct confrontation with God.

Verse 15 is very interesting, as it is a bit of a parenthesis where Jesus is speaking, stating that He is coming like a thief. This tends to remind us of a parable that Jesus taught, found in Mark 13:34-37.

"It is like a man away on a journey, who upon leaving his house and putting his slaves in charge, assigning to each one his task, also commanded the doorkeeper to stay on the alert. Therefore, be on the alert—for you do not know when the master of the house is coming, whether in the evening, at midnight, or when the rooster crows, or in the morning—in case he should come suddenly and find you asleep. What I say to you I say to all, 'Be on the alert!'"

In both cases – the passage from Revelation and the one from Mark – Jesus notes that the people of the house (of Israel) do not know when the master will return, and because of that, they should stay awake and prepared. There are many today – mostly in the Preterist and Covenant/Reformed camps – who believe that Jesus already re-turned spiritually in AD 70 when God judged the nation of Israel by causing Roman armies to destroy Jerusalem and the Temple. The problem with this interpretation is that it is simply not Scriptural. Jesus said when He returns, every eye will see Him (Matthew 24), and in Acts 1, the disciples are told (after Jesus is taken up to the clouds physically) that this Jesus would return the very same way, meaning in the clouds and physically.

2 Peter 3:4 tells us:

> *"...and saying, 'Where is the promise of His coming? For ever since the fathers fell asleep, all continues just as it was from the beginning of creation.'"*

This passage also refers to the lost, the unsaved, who have heard that Jesus is coming back so often, they see the whole thing as a joke. I can imagine it was the same in Noah's day. "Sure Noah, it's going to rain and flood the earth, and by the way, what IS rain?!"

But the future Armageddon War is merely one more proof that Jesus will return physically to this earth, and when He does, every eye will see Him because the sky will split apart like a parchment and the brightness of His coming will be far greater than the brightness of the sun. There will be no missing the event of His return.

We know that Jesus' ministry was to the house of Israel. This is not to say that He ignored those who were not of that nation. His main thrust was to call the lost house of Israel back to God. They refused and ultimately rejected Him, crucifying Him to death.

The passage in Mark is addressed to Israel. The passage in Revelation 16 is also addressed to Israel. What many do not consider is that the Tribulation period is a time when God will purify the nation of Israel and reap from them those who will make up the final remnant of Israel. These individuals (who survive the Tribulation) will be the Israelites who go into the Millennial Kingdom and receive the fullness of the Land that God originally promised to Israel through Abraham long before Israel had even been created (cf. Genesis 12, 15, 17).

Revelation 16:13-16 provides for us the details regarding Armageddon. This is the battle between God and Satan's man – the Antichrist. It is here that Satan pins all of his hopes on bringing his promises found in Isaiah 14 and Ezekiel 28 to fruition. You'll recall that Satan made five "I will" promises in Isaiah 14. He ultimately stated that he would be "like the Most High." In order for him to do this, he obviously has to overcome God Himself, something he will not be able to do.

Imagine a created being that is so narcissistic that he believes he will actually overcome God, the uncreated Being! Yet, this is the depth of Satan's ego. For Satan, everything he is currently doing that moves this earth toward the final phase of the revised Roman Empire (or the final stage of the 4th beast of Daniel 2 and 7) is to overcome God! That's what it's all about: defeating God!

God will allow Satan to do whatever it takes in his feeble attempts to bring his own promises to pass in order to prove to the entire universe (and all living things in it) that God is GOD and no one can "become" God or overthrow Him.

Armageddon

There is a war coming, the final battle between Satan and God. It's called Armageddon because it occurs on the Plain of Megiddo. As far as Satan is concerned, he has been working for thousands of years – since the time he first sinned – to get to the point of being able to rule the entire world (through his spiritual son, Antichrist), and when the moment comes for his face-to-face with God the Son, Jesus, the entire "war" is over in but a few seconds. The outcome has already been determined.

Armageddon is the climax of Satan's work to bring his promises that he swore in Isaiah 14:13-14 to fruition. You'll recall the five "I will" statements Satan made that we've already referenced.

- *I will ascend to heaven*
- *I will raise my throne above the stars of God*
- *I will sit on the mount of assembly in the recesses of the north*
- *I will ascend above the heights of the clouds*
- *I will make myself like the Most High*

Do you see how Lucifer (now Satan) promises to do several things? But notice the very last "I will" statement. It is in *that* statement that he essentially promises to become God. He will "make" himself "like the Most High."

Satan honestly believes that he can so position himself, with the help of Antichrist, the false prophet (both of Revelation 13), and all the people and armies of the earth, that he will fulfill his own promise. He will not only stand *against* God, but will be successful in *recreating* himself so that he becomes like the Most High! Is this not the height of absurdity, hubris, and complete narcissism?

But in order for the final battle known as Armageddon to occur, several things need to happen on the earth first. The 6th Bowl Judgment tells us, "*The sixth angel poured out his bowl on the great river, the Euphrates; and its water was dried up, so that the way would be prepared for the kings from the east*" (Revelation 16:12).

Notice that the direct result of the angel pouring out the contents of the 6th Bowl is that the Euphrates River dries up. Why is that? The last portion of the text tells us. It is in preparation for the kings from the east. Why? Something is going to happen. Something is being prepared.

We touched on several verses last time in which we learned that demons like frogs came out of the mouths of the dragon and the 1st and 2nd beasts. Revelation 16:15 tells us exactly what we want to know:

> *"for they are spirits of demons, performing signs, which go out to the kings of the whole world, to gather them together for the war of the great day of God, the Almighty."*

The reason these unclean spirits (demons) go out is to *deceive* the entire world (with signs, etc.) so that all the kings will gather for war against God. This is why He dries up the Euphrates River. If the leaders of the world want to fight God, He is going to give them that chance!

Notice also that the next two verses tell us, *"('Behold, I am coming like a thief. Blessed is the one who stays awake and keeps his clothes, so that he will not walk about naked and men will not see his shame.') And they gathered them together to the place which in Hebrew is called Har-Magedon."*

Why the parenthesis about God coming like a thief? This phrase refers to the Lord's Second Coming, *not* the Rapture. In other words, God is telling us through John that as preparations are being made for the world to fight God (under Satan's direction), no one still knows the exact day that Jesus will return!

In fact, I believe it is clear that Satan does not know the exact day but senses that the time is drawing close. The kings of the world probably have no clue at all and may even be wondering why they are gathering and what the ensuing war will look like.

But also consider this. People who are not ready for an event they have been told about are also "caught off guard," which is simply another way of saying that the event comes like a thief in the night. People may be aware of a specific event upcoming. They may know that it is coming, but they allow themselves to become preoccupied with other things and the event they were looking for gets put on the back burner of their mind. They start to focus on other things and lose sight of the importance of maintaining their focus on that one, upcoming, special event.

Read these words from Luke 12:45-46. "*But if that slave says in his heart, 'My master will be a long time in coming,' and begins to beat the slaves, both men and women, and to eat and drink and get drunk; the master of that slave will come on a day when he does not expect him and at an hour he does not know, and will cut him in pieces, and assign him a place with the unbelievers.*"

What happened? The slave *stopped* expecting the return of his master and began to act like an idiot, mistreating others and getting drunk. Of course, when the master *does* return, the slave is taken completely by surprise because he had stopped focusing on his master's ultimate and eventual return, even *denying* that it would happen.

This will be the world for the most part. Jesus isn't coming. God won't be back. God doesn't even exist, so how can He return to earth? It'll be a big joke, and since people will not be paying attention to the surety of this fact, when Jesus does return, they will be taken completely by surprise. Even though the people of the world – under various kings – will be gathering to fight God, they actually don't even understand why they're gathering or what they should expect! They've been so deceived by Satan that they simply do his bidding without even thinking about it.

Chapter 37

7th Bowl Judgment

We have been moving through parts of the book of Revelation highlighting the events that occur from the time the Tribulation begins until it ends. We have now arrived at the point of the Tribulation where the 7th judgment of the 3rd set of judgments occurs. Revelation 16:17-21 states the following:

> *"17 Then the seventh angel poured out his bowl upon the air, and a loud voice came out of the temple from the throne, saying, 'It is done.' 18 And there were flashes of lightning and sounds and peals of thunder; and there was a great earthquake, such as there had not been since man*

came to be upon the earth, so great an earthquake was it, and so mighty. 19 The great city was split into three parts, and the cities of the nations fell. Babylon the great was remembered before God, to give her the cup of the wine of His fierce wrath. 20 And every island fled away, and the mountains were not found. 21 And huge hail- stones, about one hundred pounds each, came down from heaven upon men; and men blasphemed God because of the plague of the hail, because its plague was extremely severe."

This is the 7th Bowl of judgment poured out by the 7th angel. When the angel states, "It is done," he is referring to the fact that the final judgment has been poured out onto the earth, not that everything is done and we have somehow arrived at the end of the action.

There are three sets of judgment in total; the Seven Seals, the Seven Trumpets, and finally, the Seven Bowls. This 7th/last Bowl represents the last of God's wrath being poured out onto the earth and those who live here. With that said, we then learn what was contained in this 7th Bowl.

As soon as the 7th Bowl is emptied out, several things begin to occur:

- Flashes of lightning and sounds of thunder
- Great earthquake (biggest the world will ever experience), mainly representing God's severe wrath on Babylon, causing:
  - The "great city" (Babylon) to split into three sections
  - The main cities of all the nations to fall
  - Every island to move away
  - Mountains to be flattened out
- 100-pound hailstones will fall
- Men curse God because of these hailstones

Imagine living during this time. Now, while it is tempting to see all of this as "figurative" or "allegorical," we need to ask ourselves if the Flood was figurative. Was the destruction of Sodom and Gomorrah real or figurative? When the sky darkened and the veil ripped from top to bottom as Jesus died on the cross – were they real or figurative?

The same people that say the above events were real and actually occurred in history will argue that the events described in Revelation 16:17-21 are figurative. Unfortunately for them, there is absolutely no reason to accept them as figurative at all.

We read the text "*every island fled away, and the mountains were not found,*" and we understand that language to be somewhat figurative or flowery. Instead of John simply saying the islands were moved and mountains collapsed because of how strong the earthquake was that was sent by God, he said it with a bit of poetic language (islands fled and mountains were not found), but this does not detract from the literalness of the statements.

We can assume that at some future point when the angel pours out the contents of the 7th Bowl judgment, the largest earthquake that this earth will ever experience will occur and flatten mountains and relocate islands. We can also assume – though the text doesn't mention it – that great tsunamis will happen because of the massive land movement.

There is no reason to understand the text any other way than literally. These things will happen as they are described. All of these things are the precursors to what takes place in Revelation 17. In this next chapter, much more detail is supplied regarding Babylon. Let's take a look, with Revelation 17:1-5.

> "*Then one of the seven angels who had the seven bowls came and spoke with me, saying, 'Come here, I will show*

*you the judgment of the great harlot who sits on many
waters, with whom the kings of the earth committed acts
of immorality, and those who dwell on the earth were
made drunk with the wine of her immorality.' And he carried me away in the Spirit into a wilderness; and I saw a
woman sitting on a scarlet beast, full of blasphemous
names, having seven heads and ten horns. The woman
was clothed in purple and scarlet, and adorned with gold
and precious stones and pearls, having in her hand a gold
cup full of abominations and of the unclean things of her
immorality, and on her forehead a name was written, a
mystery, 'BABYLON THE GREAT, THE MOTHER OF HAR-
LOTS AND OF THE ABOMINATIONS OF THE EARTH.'"*

One of the angels who held one of the Seven Bowls is given the task
of providing more information to John. He approaches John and tells
him that he will see the judgment of what the Bible calls the *"great
harlot who sits on many waters."* Clearly, the text uses *symbolism*, but
still expresses a *literal* meaning.

Harlotry in the Bible is often used as a euphemism for committing
idolatry. Whenever people worship something other than God, it is
called adultery, spiritual adultery, or harlotry. The fact that the great
harlot is sitting on many waters is a reference to the fact that she has
beguiled leaders of many nations (many waters) to commit adultery
with her. That this is not a real woman, but a spirit that causes leaders to do whatever they can to gain as much wealth and power as
possible, is clear from this reference to the "many waters," meaning
many nations and peoples.

What is the one thing that most people want today? In fact, what
have people worked for, wished for, and done all they can to gain? It
is money. Is money itself the root of all evil? No, and most people get
that wrong. Money itself is merely a tool that our economy is based
on and in order to buy or sell, some form of money is necessary. It is

not money itself, but the *"love of money is a root of all sorts of evil, and some by longing for it have wandered away from the faith and pierced themselves with many griefs"* (1 Timothy 6:10). Once you have tremendous money, you can have other things like fame, cars, expensive homes, and the rest.

It is when people love money inordinately that it becomes the object of worship. Because of that, most will do anything to gain more and to keep what they have. They will step on little people and do whatever it takes to use others to enlarge their own wealth.

Chapter 38

The Harlot

We have not really talked too much about the harlot of Revelation 17 except to say that she is able to cause men from many nations to commit spiritual adultery with her. Let's take some time to discuss the "personality" of this harlot, and we'll do so by taking another look at the text we introduced in the previous chapter from Revelation 17:1-5.

> *"1 Then one of the seven angels who had the seven bowls came and spoke with me, saying, 'Come here, I will show you the judgment of the great harlot who sits on many waters, 2 with whom the kings of the earth committed acts of immorality, and those who dwell on the earth were made drunk with the wine of her immorality.'*

> *3 And he carried me away in the Spirit into a wilderness;*
> *and I saw a woman sitting on a scarlet beast, full of blas-*
> *phemous names, having seven heads and ten horns. 4 The*
> *woman was clothed in purple and scarlet, and adorned*
> *with gold and precious stones and pearls, having in her*
> *hand a gold cup full of abominations and of the unclean*
> *things of her immorality, 5 and on her forehead a name*
> *was written, a mystery, 'BABYLON THE GREAT, THE*
> *MOTHER OF HARLOTS AND OF THE ABOMINATIONS OF*
> *THE EARTH.'"*

Like the beasts, this harlot is filled with blasphemy (v. 3). She is also sitting on a scarlet beast. This beast has seven heads and ten horns. It is the spirit of spiritual adultery that controls these ten "horns" (kings or leaders). They cannot get enough of her and drink until they're filled.

Notice in verse 4, we learn that the woman is clothed in purple and scarlet. In the Bible (as in ancient times), purple is normally associated with royalty, kingship, rulership. A person who wears purple as a ruler can also be associated with deity.

This harlot not only rides a scarlet beast (built on the blood of the saints), but is also adorned in purple (deity) and scarlet (more blood of saints). Interestingly enough today, the leaders of many areas of the world (and increasingly in America) are cracking down on Christianity. We see persecution ratcheting up in the Middle East, in Asia, and in many parts of Europe and North Africa. Sadly enough, it is also on the rise in America.

The kings (leaders) referenced in Revelation 17 have had their goal of gaining as much wealth as possible as the main reason for doing what they will do. Because of it, they have committed adultery with this woman who controls the way they think, feel, and act, from a spiritual perspective. The Bible is speaking of a spiritual force that tempts and controls men to follow the path of greed.

America is a country that was founded upon biblical principles. Many of our nation's laws come directly from the Bible. Our founding fathers were *religious,* and while people can argue about whether they were Christians or not (we know that at least a few were Deists), the plain fact of the matter is that the Bible inspired them to create a nation that was far different from England, where the Church of England and the government were in some sense married.

Our founders wanted America to be a nation where people could worship *apart* from the Church of England. They did not want government interference telling citizens what they could and could not do as far as worship was concerned. Our founders did not want a state religion.

Of course, today there is an ongoing argument about what they *really* meant and wanted. To that end, atheists tend to jump all over government (including public schools) whenever something "Christian" seems to be happening. They proclaim that there needs to be a complete separation of church and state, though this phrase does *not* appear in the United States Constitution anywhere. It came later in a separate document created by the courts.

Consider just how far society has been moved away from those Christian principles and biblical values. Not many years after the 1960s revolution took place several laws were changed in America. Prayer was no longer allowed, the Bible/Ten Commandments were removed from schools, and abortion became legal. There has been no going back since that time. I doubt seriously that we will ever be able to shut Pandora's Box and return society to some semblance of what existed before these laws in the 1970s changed the face and fabric of America forever.

It is all leading us toward the coming Tribulation in which a harlot who causes spiritual adultery in leaders will drive people even further from God. This harlot is adorned with precious stones and gold. She holds a gold cup that is filled with all sorts of abominations and immoral ideas. The saddest part is that people will not be able to get enough of it. Those who abstain will be seen as the loons of the time. They will be ridiculed, castigated, denigrated, and beaten and killed.

The very nature of people is that they do not like to be reminded when they are doing something wrong, and that happens when we don't join in with them. This is exactly what Paul means in Romans 1:32, when he says, "*and although they know the ordinance of God, that those who practice such things are worthy of death, they not only do the same, but also give hearty approval to those who practice them.*"

Not only is this harlot extremely alluring but we learn from the same passage that a name written on her forehead tells us exactly what she's like: filled with adultery and abominations. How can this be okay with God? At the same time, how can those who follow her lead be okay with God? They are not!

It won't matter how a person feels about something if God says it's wrong. All that matters is whether or not a person followed the harlot's lead. It will take more than superhuman strength to not give in. It will take God's Spirit living within the person to not give in!

But take a look at the next few verses of this same chapter in Revelation 17:6-7:

> "*6 And I saw the woman drunk with the blood of the saints, and with the blood of the witnesses of Jesus. When I saw her, I wondered greatly. 7 And the angel said to me, 'Why do you wonder? I will tell you the mystery of the*

> *woman and of the beast that carries her, which has the*
> *seven heads and the ten horns.'"*

Here we see this woman is drunk with the blood of the saints. The system of Babylon represented by the harlot is a system that is completely opposed to God. This is the reason He created ("confused") the languages of the people in Genesis 11. He knew that if He allowed them to continue on as they were, they would be able to do anything. They all spoke the same language and were one in mind and purpose. God broke it up by introducing languages (and presumably cultural identities) so that the people would be forced to go off together only in the same language groups. This put a severe wrench in Satan's desire to bring about a one-world government, one-world economy, and one-world system way back then. It meant he had to start over, from the ground up, and it has taken him thousands of years to bring us to this point.

But what we now see throughout the world is all Satan's preparation coming together, with people speaking English more than any other language. Beyond this, technology has genuinely made the world a much smaller place. What happens one minute on one side of the earth is broadcast the next minute to the other side of the earth. And yet, in spite of this, people still ask about verses in Revelation describing the return of Jesus when every eye will see Him, as if we lack the technology for the entire world to see the event at the same time!

It's important to note that this Babylon system is not only opposed to God, but because of that, it is completely opposed to those who follow Him. The spiritual forces that are behind the great harlot cannot get to God but will try to destroy those He calls His sons and daughters. Their hatred of God is so thorough that they will wage war on the saints who place their complete trust in Him. For Satan and his fallen angels, attacking the saints is the next best thing to attacking God.

The system of Babylon works so well at attacking, persecuting, and killing Christians through the ages that by the time the Tribulation rolls around, this harlot is literally drunk on the blood of the saints. This is what the world is moving toward with more and more freedoms and rights being removed from Christians. Today, Christians are seen as the bad guys, the homegrown terrorists, the ones who will allegedly stand against the federal government. Never mind that we see no evidence of this, and in fact, true conservatives (most of which are Christian) pose no threat to the government at all, but because we respect the rule of law as outlined by the US Constitution, the federal government has a problem with us. They cannot get done what they need to get done with Christians in the way.

By this point in the Tribulation, the world will have already gotten way beyond this because ten "horns" (kings) will rule the world. They will have gotten everything they wanted to get and they will be drunk with power knowing that they overcame the saints. What they do not expect, of course, is for the Antichrist to step out of the shadows at that point and take the reins.

In the latter part of verse 6, John wonders greatly. Why? What is he wondering about? Is John possibly getting caught up in the allure of the harlot? He "wondered." Never fear. He is not doing that kind of wondering, as the world does.

John is wondering why a woman – normally thought to be the more timid or weaker of the genders – is riding such a monstrous beast that controls those who lead the world! What is it about this woman that raises John's curiosity so much? The answer given to him tells us specifically that John is wondering not about the beast but primarily about the woman.

The angel then enlightens John so that he is more aware of all that the woman encompasses.

Chapter 39

Like It or Not, God is in Control

Whether or not we believe the fact that God is in control – and I do understand just how difficult it is for us at times to fully believe that He is in control – the truth of the matter is that things appear to be going along according to God's plan. If that does not place Him firmly in control, nothing does.

When I say things appear to be going according to God's plan, I'm talking about the direction society is moving, not necessarily each and every act of violence, rebellion, or suppression of truth. God's hand in all these things is overwhelmingly real. He is active, not passive. He controls the direction in which all of society is moving.

People do not seem to realize that what is happening in the world goes all the way back to Genesis 3, the events which immediately followed the fall of Adam and Eve. It was there that God rebuked our first parents and placed a curse on the earth and the animals in it. By the sweat of his brow Adam would from that day forward earn his keep. The plants of Creation would no longer give up their fruit as willingly and easily as they had done in the Garden of Eden. From the fall onward, it would take work to plant, cultivate, and harvest food to be eaten.

We may view this as harsh, but it actually saved our lives. With the fall came in the creation of the sin nature within each person. Because of the curse God placed on His Creation, the Second Law of Thermodynamics came into existence. Without having to exert energy to eat, man would die much quicker.

The animals were cursed because it was through an animal – a serpent – that Satan was able to tempt Eve successfully. Animals played a part in it, and while we may say, "Gee, that's really unfair that God would curse all the animals," it wasn't. There was no other way to do it. Everything that lives and breathes on the earth shares in the catastrophe we call "the fall."

Even though Satan was the direct cause of humankind's fall from grace, God allowed him to continue doing what he does to mankind. Why is this? In essence, God is giving Satan the opportunity to fulfill his promises (threats) made in Isaiah 14. We are all aware of Satan's (Lucifer's) five "I will" threats.

> *"I will ascend to heaven;*
> *I will raise my throne above the stars of God,*
> *And I will sit on the mount of assembly in the recesses of*
> *the north.*
> *I will ascend above the heights of the clouds;*
> *I will make myself like the Most High" (Isaiah 14:13-15)*

The above five "I wills" are at the very heart of the torturous path upon which this world was set the moment Satan was successful in causing our first parents to fail in their continued obedience to God.

In other words, there is a far larger picture of what is transpiring in the world today than simply a fully corrupt federal government in the USA. The larger picture goes well beyond black on white crime, cries of racism by blacks toward whites, and the general/specific evidences of inequality that impact this world.

Too many of us focus on specific things. Whether it's the aforementioned governmental corruption, the greed that uses capitalism to gain more wealth in spite of those who have little, or something else entirely, the real problem is beyond all of these things.

We could take the time to list many things that are happening in society that logically minded individuals would call unfair at the very least. We could count off the problems associated with Islam, Pro-Choice groups, anarchists, Marxists, self-centeredness within too many people who have been elected to lead, and more. There are simply too many things occurring in society globally that we cannot keep track of because it is a plethora. If we could focus on all of it at once, it would simply numb the mind. Even focusing on the few things we pick out among the others causes us to grow angry and even incensed at the way our government chooses to deal with citizens.

The reason it is like this is solely due to the five "I wills" in Isaiah 14 as noted above. God – in His infinite choosing – saw the heart of Satan and tells us in Isaiah 14 what was in Satan's heart. This describes the time when sin was found in Satan (Lucifer). From that point onward – immediately following Satan's fall – God determined to allow Satan the opportunities he needed to attempt to bring those five "I wills" to fruition.

Notice that the commonality with all the "I wills" is that Satan is promising that he will RULE. He says that ultimately, he "will make [him]self like the Most High." In essence, then, since the fall of Satan, God has chosen to give Satan as much room as he needs to make these promises into reality. He is giving Satan the lead he needs to try to make himself into God, very God.

This is what is behind everything we see in the world. It leads to a point where Satan will actually RULE over the entire earth. He will do so through his spiritual son, Antichrist, who will be the physical manifestation of Satan on earth. God will allow Satan's plans of world domination to come to fruition if for no other reason than to prove to Satan that even with everything going his way and with all the opportunities that God allows him to have, Satan will still lose.

This is why our government is as corrupt as it is, and in fact, this is why there is this complete air of corruption throughout the entire world presently. Globalists who have been duped into thinking that they were put here to rule over the rest of us have truly been duped. They are doing Satan's bidding (they call him Lucifer and look for his "light"), yet they believe that Satan is for them, that he wants to bless them with power and might in order to bring in a Utopia that will "bless" the entire world under their rule.

Satan is using them. God is allowing it. We are in the direct path of this coming snowball from hell. All the while that globalists believe that their god – Lucifer – desires nothing more than to bless them with unspeakable riches and power, Satan is laughing at these men for their failure to comprehend his true motives.

The upshot is this: God is giving Satan every opportunity to prove to Him (God) that he (Satan) can turn himself into eternal God and that he (Satan) will make himself like the Most High. Do you grasp the ramifications of this?

To Satan, every person on earth is but a pawn to be used for his purposes. All the while, Christ's Bride is here, on this same earth, bearing the true light to the world. Every day that the Church remains on the earth, Satan is reminded of us ultimate failure. His hatred toward true Christians seems to know no bounds. We are in his way. We are a major roadblock to his plans.

Once the Church is gone (via the Rapture), Satan will have even more freedom to do as he will. The Holy Spirit will no longer be able to work through the Church since it is gone. Yet, we also know from Scripture that starting in the middle of the Tribulation, things get even worse for all who live on this earth. Why? Because Satan can allow nothing to stand in his way to achieve the promises he uttered thousands of years ago.

I understand exactly how difficult it is to focus on what God is doing because it seems as though He isn't doing anything. Don't allow your thoughts to go there. He is busy, restraining, keeping, directing, and blessing. It is sometimes very difficult to see when there is so much going on in society that appears to negate God's work, but that is the lie of the enemy. Don't give into it.

Our job, Christian, as difficult as it may be, is to follow the directives of the apostle Paul as outlined in Ephesians 6:13.

> *"Therefore, take up the full armor of God, so that you will be able to resist in the evil day, and having done everything, to stand firm."*

We are told to have God's armor on us so that we will be able to resist. Our job is to stand resolute in God's power against the onslaught of the enemy. If there were no way to do this now, then I really don't believe the Church would still be here.

We "*have not yet resisted to the point of shedding blood in [our] striving against sin*" (Hebrews 12:4), and while we may be called upon to do that, for now, it is good to know that God is within us. If He is in us, then He is certainly for us. If He is for us, then clearly, nothing can take us out of His hand (cf. Romans 8).

1 John 4:4 clearly states:

> *"You are from God, little children, and have overcome them; because greater is He who is in you than he who is in the world."*

We have one task. That task is to place our faith in God and Him alone. Even though there are some terrible things occurring in the world today, we do not have to allow them to rob us of our peace. We can and should continue to express our faith in God and the fact that His plan, not Satan's, is what takes precedence in the end.

Trust Him. Believe Him. Have faith in His ability to save you from the doubts that attack you. Remember, this fight is already won. Satan is fully defeated, but in order to prove to the entire universe that there is no One greater than the Most High, God will allow Satan to do whatever he can to make his promises of Isaiah 14 come to pass. It will only seem that they will come to pass, but ultimately, God overrules.

Chapter 40

One Word Changes Everything

I t seems as though we are drawing so close to that final seven years of coming judgment that it can be *felt*, as though it is right around the corner. We may be closer than we realize.

We have discussed aspects of Revelation 17:1-5, dealing with the judgment of the *great harlot*. This harlot is one who has her hooks into all the nations and merchants.

That section of Revelation is pitiful because it shows to what depths of depravity humanity will stoop to feed self-centered people. Whether it's the hunting of animals for their horns (believed to be aphrodisiacs) or the wanton slaughter of millions of unborn babies per year, humanity has sunk to terribly low depths. Unfortunately, it doesn't appear as though we will bottom out until the middle of the Tribulation period.

Remember Jesus' words concerning the days of Noah in Matthew 24? We appear to be living them. Today, right is wrong and wrong is right. People are so depraved that they cannot understand when they are wrong and when they are right (if ever), but simply wait for their feelings or emotions to tell them. They play the blame game, refusing to accept any responsibility for their own misdeeds. Instead, they prefer to blame things on anyone else but themselves.

As Paul states in 2 Timothy 3:1-10, people will become lovers of themselves in the last days. From that sin flows a myriad of sins. Paul lists them: proud, disobedient, arrogant, boastful, even having a form of godliness but denying its true power. They are imitators of what it means to be a true Christian. The people of the last days who will experience the judgments of the Tribulation will be largely categorized by their self-centered natures.

Looking at Revelation 17 from an overall view, we need to understand that there are three main things happening. First, we see the results of the world following after the harlot (cf. Revelation 17:1-7). We learn not only how "she" has captivated the captains of nations, but we also learn of her final demise. The harlot represents the system of Babylon, its economy, its political system, and its religion. There comes a point when Satan – via the various world rulers, but ultimately through Antichrist, his spiritual son – will no longer have a need for the harlot (that he used to ensnare people) and the harlot will be destroyed. Revelation 18 describes Babylon's complete fall and utter failure.

Second, we learn more about the beast who was not, is, and then goes into destruction. Notice the text tells us that the beast literally comes up out of the Abyss (Revelation 17:8). This is monumental. The beast from the Abyss will literally inhabit the Antichrist for a short time (during the Tribulation) and will ultimately be destroyed, then judged, then sentenced to the Lake of Fire. This Antichrist will truly captivate the world and nearly all people will fall in line behind him. This is certainly why we see things happening in the world we cannot control. They are out of our hands. Though we *can* stand against the evil that is behind them (in the spiritual realm), we cannot change their course. It will come to pass because God will have His day of judgment.

Third, Revelation 17:14-18 tells us that the final victory belongs to the Lamb of God, Jesus, who gave Himself as a sacrifice for our sin – yours and mine. Have you received that salvation? I hope so. It comes through faith.

John the apostle is told in Revelation 17:14, "*These will wage war against the Lamb, and the Lamb will overcome them, because He is Lord of lords and King of kings, and those who are with Him are the called and chosen and faithful.*"

The Lamb will overcome all His enemies and will kill the Antichrist with a *word*. Beyond this, Jesus will deal with those who have purposefully made themselves His enemies; the time will have arrived to do so. The physical defeat of Satan will occur at this time, and while he will be allowed to try again 1,000 years later, it will also end in defeat.

There is no one who can BE God except God alone. Regardless of Satan's promises in Isaiah, he stands no chance of fulfilling them. However, God will give Satan all the opportunities he needs to attempt to bring those promises to fruition. In the end Satan will find no success because he is NOT "Lord of Lords and King of Kings"! Because of that, it is impossible that he succeeds.

All of this is leading us to the final battle – Armageddon – the battle that closes the Tribulation period with Antichrist's (Satan's) final and permanent defeat. It is absolutely tragic what is happening on the earth now, with debauchery, depravity, and death in continually increasing amounts as we move headlong toward the Tribulation.

Not only does society throughout the world suffer because of the sin nature, but the earth and animals suffer too. We are corrupted and die because of the sin nature. We die because in our first parents, we also have fallen from grace, and from that point forward the Second Law of Thermodynamics became part of our life. It happens with those we love who are family members or friends. It happens with the pets we have as well.

The Tribulation period allows sin to go to its fullest. It allows Satan to do whatever he can to bring his promises of becoming like the Most High to fruition. In the process, sin is seen for what it is and is dealt with by God's hand through one judgment after another. Yes, there is a brightness, a purity, an eternal endurance that greets us on the other side (for those who know Jesus), but getting there is the problem. I believe what we are seeing is the dramatic warm-up before the final overture begins.

I'm so glad God does not leave things there, that He shows us clearly what becomes of sin, how He judges it, and how He restores His Creation to what He intended it to be. Though judgment is on the horizon, that new day clearly follows it and, in the end, presents the greatest of all victories!

Chapter 41

Jesus is Victor!

Interestingly enough, the Bible does not end on a negative note. Then again, that all depends upon the side that you have chosen. In Revelation 19, we begin to see the coming of a new chapter to earth, led by God the Son Himself. The chapter begins with a fourfold "hallelujah!" from what is called the "great multitude" in heaven.

From there, we move onto a description of the "marriage" of the Lamb of God with His Bride, the Church. This event is followed by the return of Jesus Christ on a white horse. This section of Revelation 19:11-16 should make the hair on our necks stand up.

> *"11 And I saw heaven opened, and behold, a white horse, and He who sat on it is called Faithful and True, and in*

righteousness He judges and wages war. 12 His eyes are a
flame of fire, and on His head are many diadems; and He
has a name written on Him which no one knows except
Himself. 13 He is clothed with a robe dipped in blood, and
His name is called The Word of God. 14 And the armies
which are in heaven, clothed in fine linen, white and
clean, were following Him on white horses. 15 From His
mouth comes a sharp sword, so that with it He may strike
down the nations, and He will rule them with a rod of
iron; and He treads the wine press of the fierce wrath of
God, the Almighty. 16 And on His robe and on His thigh
He has a name written, 'KING OF KINGS, AND LORD OF
LORDS.'"

When Jesus returns, He will deal with the evil that has mounted a campaign against Holy God and His children in this world. All things will be righted and evil done away with as He clears the path with His righteousness and sword.

This is the official end of evil's reign on earth and the preparation for the start of the Millennial Reign of Jesus. Though the title deed to earth was given to the Lamb (who was found worthy to receive it) and ultimately to God the Father, it is now being put into effect. The old "owner" – Satan – has been vanquished as the new and rightful Owner arrives on the scene.

In Revelation 19:20-21 the beast and false prophet are quickly dealt with by Christ Himself and tossed into the Lake of Fire. Beginning with Revelation 20, we see that Satan himself is placed in a pit where he will remain for 1,000 years. At the end of that period, he will be released to once more attempt to revolt against God and bring his (Satan's) promises to fruition. God takes care of Satan for good at that time.

Revelation 20:11-15 highlights the Great White Throne Judgment, where all who died without Jesus as Savior will be judged. There is no chance of them receiving salvation at this point. It is here where their lives will be replayed for them. Since they rejected the only salvation available to them – made possible by Jesus Christ – their lives will be judged against the perfection and righteousness of His.

Unfortunately, everyone judged at the Great White Throne Judgment will ultimately realize that they have no hope of rescue. They are essentially being told that they have chosen to live apart from God in eternity as they chose to live apart from Him during this life.

Finally, with all the judgments, wars, and death dealt with, Jesus now turns – in Revelation 21 – to His new Creation. He creates a new earth and new heavens, fit for His Bride, which is made up of people who trusted Him in this life while they were alive.

Their reward is great, not for anything they physically did while they lived, necessarily, but for the *faith* they exercised in Jesus even though they never personally met Him, never personally heard His voice, and never personally looked into His eyes of love. It was through faith that the required spiritual transaction took place within everyone in this life who believed God, and it was counted to them as righteousness (cf. Genesis 15:6; Romans 4:3; Galatians 3:6).

God has made clear His intentions and the way of salvation. He has without equivocation told us that without faith, we cannot please Him, nor can we gain salvation (cf. Hebrews 11:6).

Beginning in Revelation 21:10-27, we learn about the New Jerusalem that God has designed and created already. It will be lowered to the new earth once it has been created.

Revelation 22 paints a picture of what heaven will be like for those who have authentically been saved. There will be no more illness or death. There will be no more sin, and in fact, because the sin nature will not exist in anyone in heaven, there will never be a chance of sinning ever again.

Think of it. No greed, no self-love, no lying, thievery, murder, or anything else that reduces humanity to something less than what God created.

Today, there is talk of a coming "new age" that is supposed to be what the "new world order" is going to usher in. We are told that this coming Utopia is something never before seen in global history, and it will finally bring peace to the whole earth for all time.

The problem is that this will never happen as long as humanity suffers from the ravages of sin caused by the sin nature within us. There is no getting around God's plan, yet this is what Satan has been attempting to accomplish since he first fell from grace.

Satan has used his intelligence, his beauty, his hatred of God (and His Creation, including people), his treachery, and everything else within his grasp and ability to try to destroy God in order to replace Him. Is it any wonder there are people in every generation who have lived under the spell of self-aggrandizement? These people have specifically opened themselves up to the enemy of our souls in order that sin might abound and become much more of a problem in society because of it.

Whenever we see someone who is so filled with narcissism and visions of grandeur, we should realize that they have given themselves over to Satan, who will use them until he's done with them. When he's done, he will simply throw them away. He's able to do this because as Paul says, he comes as an angel of light, supposedly bearing truth (cf. 2 Corinthians 11:14). Because of that, too many fall for his trappings because the sin nature within them cannot help them discern the truth.

But in spite of all this, Satan never was nor ever will be any match for Jesus. One day, Satan, along with every fallen angel and all human beings since the beginning of human history who leave this world without Jesus as Savior, will do exactly what Jesus has stated they will do, as recorded by Paul in Romans 14:11.

> *"For it is written, 'AS I LIVE, SAYS THE LORD, EVERY KNEE SHALL BOW TO ME, AND EVERY TONGUE SHALL GIVE PRAISE TO GOD.'"*

Please, above all things, do **not** leave this life without entering into a relationship with Jesus. For more information, please read the next and last chapter.

Chapter 42

Your Date with Destiny

"for all have sinned and fall short of the glory of God." – Romans 3:23

D o you know *when* you will die? Are you aware of the *day* and *hour* when you will slip from this life into eternity? I'm betting you are not privy to that information. So why are you living as if you **do** *know when it will happen?* Putting a decision about Jesus off until another day is taking a huge chance because of the fact that you do not know when you will die. That is plainly simple, and logic alone demands that you do not put this decision off. Yet you do, because the thought of becoming a Christian makes you feel uncomfortable.

You wrongly believe that to become a Christian means that you have to change in a major way *before* Jesus will accept you. It means to you giving up the things you love now because if you love them, then obviously they are wrong and God does not love them.

You are putting the cart before the horse. You must understand that God is not rejecting you. He is not standing there, tapping His foot, demanding that you eliminate those things that He does not like before you can come to Him for salvation.

If you (or anyone) could do that, you would not *need* His salvation at all. It is because you and I do things that are not pleasing to Him that we need His salvation.

What do you do that you would like to no longer do? Do you drink excessively until you cannot control it? Do you play around with drugs? Do you eat too much food until you have become overweight, lethargic, and sickly?

What other things are in your life that you do not like? Are you drawn to illicit extra-marital affairs? Do you have a problem with lust? Are you a shopaholic? Do you tend to tell lies a great deal because it makes you feel important, or to hide things about your life?

Do you find that you do not like people and you would prefer to be around animals or out in the woods than around people? Are you a workaholic? Do you place a high value on money and you find that you work very hard to obtain it?

Here's the problem. The enemy of our souls comes to us and tells us that God will never accept us until we get rid of those things. He lies to us that God essentially wants us "perfect" before He will be willing to meet us and grant us eternal life. This is completely untrue.

The other lie that our enemy tells us is that we should not become a Christian because the fun in our life will fly out the door. We will no longer be able to drink or do the fun things we enjoy now. We start to think that coming to God means becoming a doormat for people and having to fill our life with things we do not want to *ever* do.

These are all lies, and unfortunately, too many people believe them. First of all, God does not expect you to be "perfect" before you come to Him for salvation. If that were the case, no one would be able to ever approach Him.

Secondly, God does not say that He is going to take away all the things we enjoy and replace them with things we hate. What is wrong with enjoying the lake on your boat? What is wrong with spending a day with the family fishing or just relaxing in the mountains? There is nothing wrong with these things.

What God *will* do is begin to remove the things that have ensnared you so that life is actually draining from you, but you are not aware of it. For instance, maybe you drink excessively and you have tried everything you can think of to quit. You have gone to AA meetings, spent thousands of dollars on this program or that, and you have even used your own will power to free yourself from the addiction to alcohol, all to no avail.

The question is not: *do I need to quit before I come to Jesus*? The question is: *am I willing to allow Him to work in and through me to take away the addiction I have to alcohol*? Do you see the difference? Are you willing to allow Him to work in you to break that addiction so that you will become a healthier person, one who is able to think straight and one who learns to rely on Him for strength? That is all He wants you to be able to do. He knows you cannot break that addiction (or any addiction for that matter) with your own strength and willpower. Are you willing to allow Him to do it in and through you?

What if you are a workaholic? What if you have "things" like a boat, a house in Cancun, a large bank account, four cars, and more? Do you think that God is going to ask you to give it up, or worse, do you think that God will simply come in and take all of that from you? I know of nothing in Scripture that tells us He will do that.

What God will do with all of those who come to Him trusting Him for salvation is one thing, which begins the moment we receive salvation and will continue until the day we stand before Him. He will begin to create within us the character of Jesus (cf. Ephesians 2:10).

Here is a verse from the Old Testament that was said originally through the prophet Ezekiel to the people of Israel. While this was specifically stated to the Jews, it is applicable to all who receive salvation through Jesus Christ.

"Moreover, I will give you a new heart and put a new spirit within you; and I will remove the heart of stone from your flesh and give you a heart of flesh. I will put My Spirit within you and cause you to walk in My statutes, and you will be careful to observe My ordinances." (Ezekiel 36:26-27).

God is speaking here through Ezekiel, and He is saying that He will give the people a new heart of flesh, removing that old heart of stone. This is God's responsibility. God is the One who makes that happen. We are told in the book of Hebrews that God is the Author and Finisher of our faith (cf. Hebrews 12:2). This tells me that God is the One who changes me from within so that over time, my desires are slowly turned into His desires.

I recall years ago thinking that God wanted to do everything in my life that I did not want Him to do. I fell into the asinine belief that He wanted to change everything about me. What I learned is that yes, there are things that God does want to change about me. However, there is a lot that God originally gave me that He has also enhanced and used for His glory.

Maybe you are a workaholic who thinks that working hard is something God does not want you to do. This is not necessarily the case. He may have given you the ability and the knowledge to work in the area of finance for a great purpose. All He may wind up doing is dialing back your workaholic tendencies so that you have more time to enjoy your family and study His Word.

But you say you smoke, or drink, or use illegal drugs, and you don't want to give those up. As I stated, you can't give those up under your own power, and the fact that you have tried so many times has proven it to you.

But God knows what is and what is not good for you. Are you willing to *allow* Him to work in you to change your desires so that you no longer want to smoke, use illegal drugs, or drink nearly as much?

Then you say that you believe God wants to make you a Christian so you can become miserable. Isn't that what most Christians are: miserable? Not the Christians I know, and certainly not me, my wife, or our children.

Where does the Bible say that God wants us miserable? You will not find it. What God wants is for us to be blessed, and that begins when we receive salvation from His hand.

You know, if we would stop and take the time to consider the fact that this life is exceedingly short if we compare it to eternity, we will then realize that there is nothing so important that it should keep us from receiving Jesus as Savior and Lord.

Unfortunately, too many people do not consider the brevity of life. They think they will live forever, or at the very least, that they will die when they are really old and gray. That will come too soon. Even though I have just recently turned 58, it truly seems like yesterday that I was a young boy fishing in the Delaware River near Hobart, New York. There I spent many Saturdays fishing and simply enjoying being outdoors. How did life go by so very quickly? How could that have happened?

It has happened and I am at a point in life where not only do I realize that this life is short, but I actually look forward to spending eternity with Jesus after this life. Does that sound morbid to you? It shouldn't, because by comparing this life to eternity, we should get a sense of what is truly important.

God does not expect us to become Mother Theresas. He does not necessarily expect us to give up everything and become missionaries in Outer Mongolia. What God expects is for us to simply allow Him to change our character as He sees fit.

Over time, we may well find that we have simply stopped swearing without realizing it. Our desire for cigarettes or alcohol has nearly evaporated. Illicit affairs no longer enter the picture.

We also may find that some of the things we want to eliminate in our life become more pronounced. Often the enemy will do this to cause us to focus on something that God is not even doing in our lives at that point. It causes tension, frustration, and self-anger.

If you have gotten to this point in your life and you have not dealt with the question about Jesus, it is about time you do so. You need to stop what you are doing and realize a couple of things before you go through another minute in this life.

- **Sinner**: you need to realize that you are a sinner. You have sinned and you will continue to sin. Sin is breaking the laws that God has set up. We all sin. We have all broken God's laws and that breaks any connection we might have had with God. Sin pushes us away from Him.

  Romans 3:23 says, "*For all have sinned, and come short of the glory of God.*" That means you and that means me. All means all. That is the first step. We need to recognize and agree with God that yes, we are sinners. I'm a sinner. You are a sinner. This results in God's anger, what the Bible terms "wrath."

- **God's Wrath**: Romans 1:18 says, "*For the wrath of God is revealed from heaven against all ungodliness and unrighteousness of men who suppress the truth in unrighteousness.*"

This is as much a fact as the truth that we are all sinners. Because we are sinners – by breaking God's law(s) – God has every right to be angry with us and ultimately destroy that which is sinful. If we choose to remain "in" our sinful states throughout this life, we will – unfortunately – be destroyed with the rest of sin.

Fortunately, there *is* a remedy, and it is salvation.

- **God's Gift**: In the 16th chapter of Acts, a jailer asks Paul this famous question: *what must I do to be saved?* The question was asked because Paul and Barnabas had been imprisoned, and while there, they began singing praises to God.

God then sent a powerful earthquake that opened the doors to all the prison cells, yet no one escaped. When the jailer arrived, he saw that everyone was still in their cells, and after seeing that miracle (what prisoner would not want to escape from prison?), turned and asked what he must do to be saved. He was speaking of the spiritual aspect of things. He wanted to know how he could be guaranteed eternal life.

The answer Paul gave the man was, "*They said, "Believe in the Lord Jesus, and you will be saved, you and your household."* (Acts 16:31).

This is not head knowledge or intellectual assent. This is *believing from the heart.* In fact, Paul makes a very similar statement in another book he wrote, Romans. He says, "*that if you confess with your mouth Jesus as Lord, and believe in your heart that God raised Him from the dead, you will be saved; for with the heart a person believes, resulting in righteousness, and with the mouth he confesses, resulting in salvation,*" (Romans 10:9-10).

When we fully believe something, we confess that it is true. It must begin in the heart because that is where the will is located. We must want to believe. We must endeavor to believe. We must seek to believe.

We must stop giving ourselves all the reasons to deny or ignore Jesus. As God, He became a Man, born of a virgin. He clothed Himself with humanity that He might show us how to live, and in so doing, He would keep every portion of the law.

If Jesus was capable of keeping every portion of the law, then He would be found worthy to become a sacrifice for our sin – yours and mine. If He became a sacrifice for our sin, then all that we must do is embrace Him and His sacrificial death.

In short then, to become saved we must:

1. Admit (we sin)
2. Repent (want to turn away from it)
3. Believe (that Jesus is the answer)
4. Embrace (the truth about Jesus)

We **admit** that we are a sinner, that we have sinned. This is nothing more than agreeing with God that we have broken His law. Can you honestly say that you have not broken God's law? If you admit to breaking even the "smallest" law, then you are a lawbreaker.

After we admit that we have sinned, the next step is found in **repenting**. Some believe that repenting is actually moving away from sin. This author believes that it is a willingness to move away from sin, and there is a difference.

As we have already discussed, it is impossible to stop sinning. Human beings simply cannot do it because as long as we live, we will have a sin nature, which is something within us that gives us a propensity to sin. As long as we have this inner propensity to sin or break God's laws, we will never be perfect in this life.

We cannot one day say, "Lord, I promise to stop sinning." If we do that, we are only kidding ourselves and setting ourselves up for major failure. We cannot stop sinning in this life. The most we can do is *want* to stop sinning and then spend the rest of our lives allowing God to create the character of Jesus within us, slowly, little by little.

Repenting is to decide that you no longer want to do the things that keep us out of heaven. We no longer wish to break God's laws. It is not promising God that we will never sin again.

Once we admit, then repent, we must **believe**. This is one of the most difficult things to do because believing that Jesus died in our place, that He lived a perfectly sinless life, is extremely difficult. Our minds cannot grasp that truth. We must ask God to open our eyes to that truth so that we can embrace it.

While on the cross next to Jesus, the one thief joined the other thief in ridiculing Jesus. Then, all of a sudden – as we read in Luke 23:42-43 – this same thief that had just been ridiculing Him now turned to Him with a new understanding.

It was this new understanding that prompted the thief to say to Jesus, *"Jesus, remember me when You come in Your kingdom!"* Jesus looked at the man and responded to him, *"Truly I say to you, today you shall be with Me in Paradise."*

What had occurred in the mind and heart of that thief from one moment to the next? One thing, and that one thing was that God opened the thief's eyes so that he could see the truth. It was as if the blinders fell off and he now saw and understood who Jesus was, even to the most cursory degree that Jesus was dying not for Himself, but for others.

It was this understanding, this awareness, which prompted the man to ask Jesus to simply be remembered. Jesus went way beyond it to promise the man that he would be with Jesus that day in paradise.

Please notice in Luke 23 that there is nothing in the chapter that tells us that the man promised Jesus he would give up sin, or that he would never sin again. There is nothing that tells us that thief took the time to enter into a final deathbed confession of his sins so that he could be absolved.

The thief made no promises to Jesus at all. What he experienced was the truth of who Jesus was and what Jesus accomplished for humanity. Jesus accomplished what we cannot. What is left is for each person to *admit, repent, believe,* and *embrace.*

Let me clarify here that though we do not see any verbal repentance from the thief, we know that he did repent. He admitted as well. How can we know this? Simply due to the thief's complete about-face with respect to his attitude toward Jesus. One minute, he was ridiculing Jesus, and the next, embracing Him. This is important. There is no way he could have or would have *embraced* Jesus had he not been humbled by the truth *about* Jesus.

Once the thief saw the truth, he was instantly humbled. Within himself, he knew that he was a sinner, and in fact the text states that this is what he told the other thief dying next to him. *"But the other answered, and rebuking him said, "Do you not even fear God, since you are under the same sentence of condemnation? And we indeed are suffering justly, for we are receiving what we deserve for our deeds; but this man has done nothing wrong."* (Luke 23:40-41). Something happened within the heart of the one thief. In one moment, the thief went from harassing Jesus to recognizing his own sinfulness and then ultimately asking for grace, which was freely given to him.

Whether he said it or not, the thief went from haughtiness to humility in a very short space of time, and it was all because he saw the truth about Jesus. That truth helped him realize that he deserved his death and what would happen to him after death. He understood that Jesus did not deserve death.

From here, the thief fully embraced the truth about Jesus and was rewarded with eternal life because of it. He did not come off the cross to be water baptized. He did not list a long litany of offenses against God. He recognized the truth about Jesus, was humbled, and embraced that truth!

This is what each of us needs to do. We cannot give in to the lie that tells us that we are not good enough or we have not given up enough before God will accept us. We must reject the lie that says we must somehow earn our salvation.

Jesus has done everything that is necessary to make salvation available to us. The only thing that is left for us is to see the truth. Once we see that truth, it should humble us to the point of embracing Jesus and all that He stands for and is to us.

The 8th chapter of Romans begins with the fact that all who trust Jesus for salvation are no longer condemned...*ever*. All of my sins –

past, present, and future – have not only been forgiven, but canceled. It is because of my faith in the atonement (death) of Jesus that God is able to cancel all of my sins, even the ones that I have not committed yet. This does not make me eager to commit them. It makes me want to do what I can to avoid sinning.

If you do not know Jesus, please do not put down this book without deliberately *believing* that He is God, that He died for you by the shedding of His blood on the cross, that He rose three days later because death could not keep Him. Do you believe that? If you do not yet believe it, do you *want* to believe it? If so, then simply ask God to help you come to believe all that Jesus is and all that He has accomplished for you. God will answer your prayers and you may either receive instantaneous awareness of all that Jesus is and has done, or it may be a *growing* awareness over time. In either case, it is the most important decision you will ever make.

Turn to Him now and pray for knowledge of the truth and an ability to embrace it. Please. He is waiting for you.

Ask Yourself:

1. Do you *know* Jesus? Are you in *relationship* with Him? Have you had a spiritual transaction according to John 3?
2. Do you *want* to receive eternal life through the only salvation that is available?
3. Do you believe that Jesus is God the Son, who was born of a virgin, lived a sinless life, died a bloody and gruesome death to pay for your sin, was buried, and rose again on the third day? Do you *believe* this?
4. Do you *want* to *embrace* the truth from #3?
5. Pray that God will open your eyes and provide you with the faith to begin believing the truth about Jesus. Ask Him to help your faith embrace the truth, realizing that you are not good

enough to save yourself and that your sin will keep you out of God's Kingdom without His salvation.

6. Pray as if your life depended upon it because *it does*!

Keep up with us at Study-Grow-Ministries:
http://www.studygrowknow.com

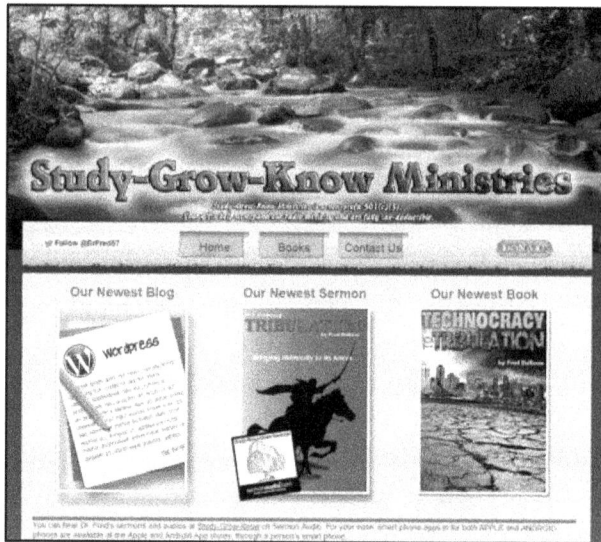

and listen to our weekly messages at:
http://www.sermonaudio.com/studygrowknow

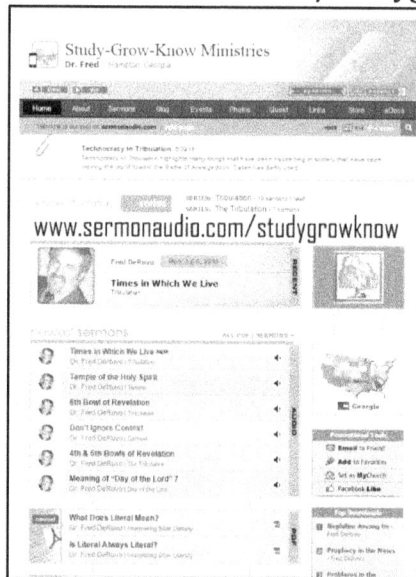

www.ingramcontent.com/pod-product-compliance
Lightning Source LLC
Chambersburg PA
CBHW081510040426
42447CB00013B/3173